Huggable Amigurumi

18 Cute and Cuddly Animal Softies

Shannen Nicole Chua

Martingale
Create with Confidence

Dedication
To Anielle and Acho

Huggable Amigurumi: 18 Cute and Cuddly Animal Softies
© 2016 by Shannen Nicole Chua

Martingale®
19021 120th Ave. NE, Ste. 102
Bothell, WA 98011-9511 USA
ShopMartingale.com

No part of this product may be reproduced in any form, unless otherwise stated, in which case reproduction is limited to the use of the purchaser. The written instructions, photographs, designs, projects, and patterns are intended for the personal, noncommercial use of the retail purchaser and are under federal copyright laws; they are not to be reproduced by any electronic, mechanical, or other means, including informational storage or retrieval systems, for commercial use. Permission is granted to photocopy patterns for the personal use of the retail purchaser. Attention teachers: Martingale encourages you to use this book for teaching, subject to the restrictions stated above.

The information in this book is presented in good faith, but no warranty is given nor results guaranteed. Since Martingale has no control over choice of materials or procedures, the company assumes no responsibility for the use of this information.

Printed in China
21 20 19 18 17 16   8 7 6 5 4 3 2 1

Library of Congress Cataloging-in-Publication Data is available upon request.

ISBN: 978-1-60468-844-3

MISSION STATEMENT
We empower makers who use fabric and yarn to make life more enjoyable.

CREDITS

PUBLISHER AND CHIEF VISIONARY OFFICER
Jennifer Erbe Keltner

CONTENT DIRECTOR
Karen Costello Soltys

DESIGN MANAGER
Adrienne Smitke

MANAGING EDITOR
Tina Cook

COVER AND INTERIOR DESIGNER
Regina Girard

ACQUISITIONS EDITOR
Karen M. Burns

PHOTOGRAPHER
Brent Kane

TECHNICAL EDITOR
Amy Polcyn

ILLUSTRATORS
Rose Wright
Linda Schmidt

COPY EDITOR
Marcy Heffernan

Contents

4 » Introduction

5 » Belle Bluebird
8 » Henry Elephant
11 » Sofie Swan
14 » Lila, Littlun's Lamb
17 » Mia Bunny
20 » Connor Frog
23 » Brian Turtle
26 » Elliott Giraffe
29 » Moby Whale
32 » Monty Monkey
35 » Tommy Turkey
38 » Snowie Owl
41 » George Lion
44 » Stella Squirrel
47 » Sammie Seal
50 » Ellie Penguin
53 » Rocco Raccoon
56 » Gunny Bear

60 » Crochet Basics
63 » Abbreviations
64 » About the Author
64 » Acknowledgments

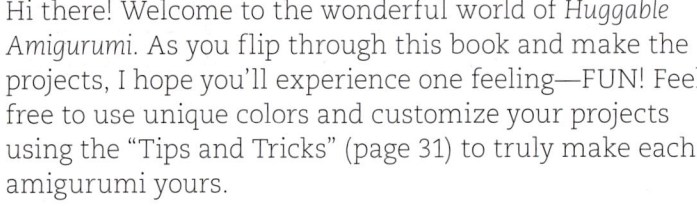

Introduction

Hi there! Welcome to the wonderful world of *Huggable Amigurumi*. As you flip through this book and make the projects, I hope you'll experience one feeling—FUN! Feel free to use unique colors and customize your projects using the "Tips and Tricks" (page 31) to truly make each amigurumi yours.

   I've tried to fill this book with various projects that use different styles of making an amigurumi, from basic egg-shaped bodies to more realistic versions and even a more cartoon-like approach. I hope that you will see how easy making amigurumi is and that you will L-O-V-E it!

   I, together with the amazing team at Martingale, have worked very hard to make sure that this book is everything you want and more. Working late nights, doing multiple proofreads, and everything in between—all of those hardships were so very worth doing, as shown by this finished book.

   If you ever want to share your own work using the patterns and tricks you find here, feel free to tag me on Instagram or Twitter @SNCxCreations or even post it to my Facebook wall. I'd love to see the wonderful toys you make!

Shannen

» Belle Bluebird »

What better way to start this book than with a bluebird in the sweetest shades of blue! With her simple pattern and basic color changes, Belle will be ready to chirp along as your new singing buddy in no time.

Huggable Amigurumi

> **Skill Level:** Easy
> **Finished Size:** 9" tall

Materials

See page 60 for more about yarns.

Yarn:

Light worsted- or DK-weight 4-ply acrylic yarn

120 yds in powder blue for head, body, and tail

10 yds in sky blue for top feathers, wings, and tummy

6 yds in blue for wings and flower

4 yds in yellow gold for beak

4 yds in cream for tummy

2 yds in moss green for vines

Hooks and Notions:

US Size F-5 (3.75 mm) crochet hook

2 buttons, 20 mm diameter, for eyes

Stitch marker, fiberfill stuffing, tapestry needle

Flower Crown

For flower, with blue, make a magic circle (page 61).

Rnd 1: Work 6 sc in ring.

Rnd 2: *Sc 2 in next sc; rep from * around—12 sts.

Rnd 3: *Dc 4 in same st, sl st in next st; rep from * 6 times—30 sts.

Fasten off, leaving a long tail for sewing.

For vine, with moss green, ch 62 for foundation ch, join in a ring. Sl st in next 12 ch, [sl st in next 4 ch, ch 4, sc in 2nd st from hook and in next 2 ch (leaf made), sl st in next ch of foundation ch] 7 times, sl st in last 15 ch.

Fasten off.

Bird

The bird is assembled from multiple pieces, including feathers, wings, a head, tummy, and so on.

TOP FEATHERS

With sky blue, ch 15.

Sc in 2nd ch from hook and in next 2 ch, *ch 4, sc in 2nd st from hook and in next 2 ch (feather made), sl st in next ch of foundation ch; rep from * to end.

Fasten off, leaving a long tail for sewing.

WINGS

Make 2.

With sky blue, make a magic circle.

Rnd 1: Work 6 sc in ring.

Rnd 2: *Sc 2 in next sc; rep from * around—12 sts.

Rnd 3: (Sc in next st, 2 sc in following st) 6 times—18 sts.

Rnd 4: (Sc in each of next 2 sts, 2 sc in following st) 6 times—24 sts.

Rnd 5: (Sc in each of next 3 sts, 2 sc in following st) 6 times—30 sts.

Rnd 6: With blue, sc in next st, 2 hdc in next st, hdc in next st, [(2 dc, ch 1, 2 dc) in same st, sk next st, sl st in next st] twice, (2 dc, ch 1, 2 dc) in same st, hdc in next st, 2 hdc in next st, sc in each of rem 18 sts—42 sts.

Fasten off, leaving a long tail for sewing.

TUMMY

With cream, make a magic circle.

Rnd 1: Work 7 sc in ring.

Belle's wings are made from two yarn colors.

Tail view.

Top-down view of Belle's head feather.

Rnd 2: *Sc 2 in next sc; rep from * around—14 sts.

Rnd 3: Sc in each of first 4 sts, 2 sc in each of next 7 sts, sc in each of rem 3 sts—21 sts.

Rnd 4: Sc in each of first 3 sts, (sc in next st, 2 sc in next st) 7 times, sc in each of rem 4 sts—28 sts.

Rnd 5: Hdc in each of first 3 sts, (hdc in each of next 3 sts, 2 hdc in next st) 7 times, hdc in each of rem 4 sts—35 sts.

Rnd 6: With sky blue, (sc in each of next 4 sts, 2 sc in following st) 7 times—42 sts.

Rnd 7: (Sc in each of next 5 sts, 2 sc in following st) 7 times—49 sts.

Fasten off, leaving a long tail for sewing.

BEAK

With yellow gold, make a magic circle.

Rnd 1: Work 5 sc in ring.

Rnd 2: *Sc 2 in next sc; rep from * around—10 sts.

Rnd 3: (Sc in next st, 2 sc in following st) 5 times—15 sts.

Rnd 4: Sc around.

Rnd 5: (Sc in each of next 2 sts, 2 sc in following st) 5 times—20 sts.

Fasten off, leaving a long tail for sewing.

TAIL

With powder blue, make a magic circle.

Row 1: Work 6 sc in ring, turn. Do not join.

Row 2: Ch 3 (counts as dc), (dc, ch 1, 2 dc) in first st, sl st in next st, [(2 dc, ch 1, 2 dc) in same st, sl st in next st] 2 times. Fasten off, leaving a long tail for sewing.

HEAD AND BODY

With powder blue, make a magic circle.

Rnd 1: Work 6 sc in ring.

Rnd 2: (Sc in each of next 2 sts, 2 sc in following st) 2 times—8 sts.

Rnd 3: *Sc 2 in next sc; rep from * around—16 sts.

Rnd 4: (Sc in next st, 2 sc in following st) 8 times—24 sts.

Rnd 5: Sc around.

Rnd 6: (Sc in each of next 2 sts, 2 sc in following st) 8 times—32 sts.

Rnd 7: (Sc in each of next 3 sts, 2 sc in following st) 8 times—40 sts.

Rnd 8: (Sc in each of next 4 sts, 2 sc in following st) 8 times—48 sts.

Rnd 9: (Sc in each of next 7 sts, 2 sc in following st) 6 times—54 sts.

Sew top feathers in place on head, wrapping in a spiral from rnds 1–5 of head.

Rnds 10–21: Sc around.

Rnd 22: (Sc in each of next 7 sts, sc2tog) 6 times—48 sts.

Rnd 23: (Sc in each of next 6 sts, sc2tog) 6 times—42 sts.

Rnd 24: (Sc in each of next 5 sts, sc2tog) 6 times—36 sts.

Rnd 25: (Sc in each of next 4 sts, sc2tog) 6 times—30 sts.

Rnd 26: (Sc in each of next 3 sts, sc2tog) 6 times—24 sts.

Rnd 27: (Sc in each of next 2 sts, sc2tog) 6 times—18 sts.

Rnd 28: Sc around.

Sew eyes in place at rnds 18–21, leaving 10 sts between them. Sew beak 2 sts away from each eye between rnds 20 and 25.

Rnd 29: (Sc in each of next 5 sts, 2 sc in following st) 3 times—21 sts.

Rnd 30: (Sc in each of next 6 sts, 2 sc in following st) 3 times—24 sts.

Rnd 31: (Sc in each of next 3 sts, 2 sc in following st) 6 times—30 sts.

Rnds 32 and 33: Sc around.

Rnd 34: (Sc in each of next 4 sts, 2 sc in following st) 6 times—36 sts.

Rnds 35–38: Sc around.

Rnd 39: (Sc in each of next 5 sts, 2 sc in following st) 6 times—42 sts.

Rnds 40–42: Sc around.

Rnd 43: (Sc in each of next 6 sts, 2 sc in following st) 6 times—48 sts.

Rnds 44 and 45: Sc around.

Rnd 46: (Sc in each of next 6 sts, sc2tog) 6 times—42 sts.

Rnd 47: (Sc in each of next 5 sts, sc2tog) 6 times—36 sts.

Rnd 48: (Sc in each of next 4 sts, sc2tog) 6 times—30 sts.

Rnd 49: (Sc in each of next 3 sts, sc2tog) 6 times—24 sts.

Rnd 50: (Sc in each of next 2 sts, sc2tog) 6 times—18 sts.

Rnd 51: (Sc in next st, sc2tog) 6 times—12 sts.

Rnd 52: Sc in every other st—6 sts.

Fasten off, leaving a long tail for sewing.

» Assembly

Sew tummy to body. Sew tail in place, near rnd 30. Sew flower to vines and sew in place on head. Sew wings to body.

Stuff. Weave in ends.

» Henry Elephant »

Elephants are normally gray, but little Henry here is all white with accents of blue. Suited up with his fabulous minty green collar, he's ready for a day around town! His pattern is all about simple shapes and pops of color.

Henry Elephant

Skill Level: Easy
Finished Size: 11" tall

» Materials

See page 60 for more about yarns.

Yarn:
Light worsted- or DK-weight 4-ply acrylic yarn
180 yds in white for body
45 yds in blue for trim
3 yds in green for collar

Hooks and Notions:
US Size F-5 (3.75 mm) crochet hook
2 buttons, 20 mm diameter, for eyes
Stitch marker, fiberfill stuffing, tapestry needle

» Trunk

With white, make a magic circle (page 61).

Rnd 1: Work 4 sc in ring.

Rnd 2: *Sc 2 in next sc; rep from * around—8 sts.

Rnd 3: (Sc in next st, 2 sc in following st) 4 times—12 sts.

Rnd 4: (Sc in each of next 2 sts, 2 sc in following st) 4 times—16 sts.

Rnd 5: Through back loops only, sc around.

Rnds 6–8: Sc around.

Rnd 9: (Sc in each of next 2 sts, sc2tog) 4 times—12 sts.

Rnds 10–14: Sc around.

Rnds 15 and 16: Sl st 6 times, sc in each of rem 6 sts—12 sts.

Rnd 17: (Sc in next st, 2 sc in following st) 6 times—18 sts.

Fasten off, leaving a long tail for sewing.

» Inner Ears

Make 2.

With blue, ch 13.

Rnd 1: Sc in 2nd st from hook and in each ch across. Turn foundation ch. On opposite side of foundation ch, sc in each ch—24 sts.

Rnd 2: (Sc in each of next 3 sts, 2 sc in following st) 6 times—30 sts.

Rnd 3: (Sc in each of next 5 sts, 2 sc in following st) 5 times—35 sts.

Rnd 4: Sc in each of next 15 sts, 2 sc in each of next 5 sts, sc in each of rem 15 sts—40 sts.

Fasten off, leaving a long tail for sewing.

» Outer Ears

Make 2.

With white, ch 17.

Rnd 1: Sc in 2nd st from hook and in each ch to end. Turn foundation ch. On opposite side of foundation ch, sc in each ch—32 sts.

Rnd 2: (Sc in each of next 3 sts, 2 sc in following st) 8 times—40 sts.

Rnd 3: (Sc in each of next 7 sts, 2 sc in following st) 5 times—45 sts.

Rnd 4: (Sc in each of next 8 sts, 2 sc in following st) 5 times—50 sts.

Rnd 5: Sc in each of next 20 sts, 2 sc in each of next 10 sts, sc in each of rem 20 sts—60 sts.

Fasten off, leaving a long tail for sewing.

Using yarn tail of inner ear, sew inner ear to outer ear.

The collar is crocheted separately and attached during finishing.

» Collar

With green, ch 32.

Row 1: Hdc in 3rd ch from hook and in each ch to end, turn—30 sts.

Row 2: Ch 3 (counts as dc), 2 dc in same st, sl st in next st, (3 dc in next st, sl st in next st) 13 times—2 sts rem unworked. Fasten off.

» Arms

Make 2.

With blue, make a magic circle.

Rnd 1: Work 6 sc in ring.

Rnd 2: *Sc 2 in next sc; rep from * around—12 sts.

Rnd 3: (Sc in next st, 2 sc in following st) 6 times—18 sts.

Rnd 4: (Sc in each of next 2 sts, 2 sc in following st) 6 times—24 sts.

Rnds 5–8: Sc around.

Rnd 9: With white, sc around.

Rnd 10: (Sc in each of next 2 sts, sc2tog) 6 times—18 sts.

Rnds 11–15: Sc around.

Rnd 16: (Sc in next st, sc2tog) 6 times—12 sts.

Rnds 17–21: Sc around.

Fasten off, leaving a long tail for sewing.

» Head and Body

With white, make a magic circle.

Rnd 1: Work 7 sc in ring.

Rnd 2: *Sc 2 in next sc; rep from * around—14 sts.

Rnd 3: (Sc in next st, 2 sc in following st) 7 times—21 sts.

Rnd 4: (Sc in each of next 2 sts, 2 sc in following st) 7 times—28 sts.

Rnd 5: (Sc in each of next 3 sts, 2 sc in following st) 7 times—35 sts.

Rnd 6: (Sc in each of next 4 sts, 2 sc in following st) 7 times—42 sts.

Rnd 7: (Sc in each of next 5 sts, 2 sc in following st) 7 times—49 sts.

Rnds 8–18: Sc around.

Rnd 19: (Sc in each of next 6 sts, 2 sc in following st) 7 times—56 sts.

Rnd 20: Sc around.

Rnd 21: (Sc in each of next 6 sts, sc2tog) 7 times—49 sts.

Rnd 22: (Sc in each of next 5 sts, sc2tog) 7 times—42 sts.

Rnd 23: (Sc in each of next 4 sts, sc2tog) 7 times—35 sts.

Rnd 24: (Sc in each of next 3 sts, sc2tog) 7 times—28 sts.

Rnd 25: (Sc in each of next 2 sts, sc2tog) 7 times—21 sts.

Stuff trunk and sew to head. Sew eyes in place 3 or 4 sts away from trunk on each side. Sew ears to head using tail of outer ear.

Rnds 26 and 27: Sc around.

Rnd 28: (Sc in each of next 2 sts, 2 sc in following st) 7 times—28 sts.

Rnd 29: Sc around.

Rnd 30: (Sc in each of next 3 sts, 2 sc in following st) 7 times—35 sts.

Rnds 31 and 32: Sc around.

Rnd 33: (Sc in each of next 4 sts, 2 sc in following st) 7 times—42 sts.

Rnds 34–39: Sc around.

Rnd 40: (Sc in each of next 5 sts, 2 sc in following st) 7 times—49 sts.

Rnds 41–43: Sc around.

Rnd 44: (Sc in each of next 5 sts, sc2tog) 7 times—42 sts.

Rnd 45: (Sc in each of next 4 sts, sc2tog) 7 times—35 sts.

Rnd 46: (Sc in each of next 3 sts, sc2tog) 7 times—28 sts.

Rnd 47: (Sc in each of next 2 sts, sc2tog) 7 times—21 sts.

Rnd 48: (Sc in each of next 5 sts, sc2tog) 3 times—18 sts.

Rnd 49: (Sc in each of next 4 sts, sc2tog) 3 times—15 sts.

Rnd 50: (Sc in next st, sc2tog) 5 times—10 sts.

Rnd 51: Sc in every other st—5 sts.

Fasten off, leaving a long tail for sewing.

» Toes

Make 6.

With blue, make a magic circle.

Rnd 1: Work 5 sc in ring.

Rnd 2: *Sc 2 in next sc; rep from * around—10 sts.

Fasten off, leaving a long tail for sewing.

» Legs

Make 2.

With white, make a magic circle.

Rnd 1: Work 6 sc in ring.

Rnd 2: *Sc 2 in next sc; rep from * around—12 sts.

Rnd 3: (Sc in next st, 2 sc in following st) 6 times—18 sts.

Rnd 4: (Sc in each of next 2 sts, 2 sc in following st) 6 times—24 sts.

Rnd 5: (Sc in each of next 3 sts, 2 sc in following st) 6 times—30 sts.

Rnds 6–9: Sc around.

Sew 3 toes to the bottom of each leg.

Rnd 10: (Sc in each of next 3 sts, sc2tog) 6 times—24 sts.

Rnds 11–15: Sc around.

Rnd 16: (Sc in each of next 4 sts, sc2tog) 4 times—20 sts.

Rnds 17–21: Sc around.

Rnd 22: (Sc in each of next 3 sts, sc2tog) 4 times—16 sts.

Rnds 23–25: Sc around.

Fasten off, leaving a long tail for sewing.

» Assembly

Wrap collar around neck, overlapping by 2 sts and sew tog. Sew arms in place. Sew legs in place. Weave in ends.

For tail, cut 3 pieces of white yarn, each 5" long. With tapestry needle, thread each through body and tie tog with an overhand knot.

» Sofie Swan »

Swans are elegant and regal, and what better way to capture that than with a delicate purple cygnet topped with a crown! With little Sofie, you don't need to worry about sewing together a lot of different parts.

Huggable Amigurumi

> **Skill Level:** Easy
> **Finished Size:** 9½" tall

» Materials

See page 60 for more about yarns.

Yarn:

Light worsted- or DK-weight 4-ply acrylic yarn (3)

180 yds in purple for head and body

45 yds in cream for wings

25 yds in yellow gold for crown and beak

Hooks and Notions:

US Size F-5 (3.75 mm) crochet hook

2 safety eyes, 15 mm diameter

Stitch marker, fiberfill stuffing, tapestry needle

» Crown

With yellow gold, ch 55, join in a ring.

Rnd 1: Hdc in each ch around—55 sts.

Rnd 2: Hdc around.

Row 3: Sc in each of next 24 sts, hdc in next st, 2 dc in next st, 3 dc in next st, ch 3, sl st in base of ch-3 (picot made), sk next st, 3 dc in next st, 2 dc in next st, hdc in next st, sc in each of rem 24 sts—60 sts. Fasten off.

» Beak

With yellow gold, make a magic circle (page 61).

Rnd 1: Work 5 sc in ring.

Rnd 2: *Sc 2 in next sc; rep from * around—10 sts.

Rnd 3: (Sc in next st, 2 sc in following st) 5 times—15 sts.

Rnd 4: Sc around.

Rnd 5: (Sc in each of next 2 sts, 2 sc in following st) 5 times—20 sts.

Rnd 6: Sc around.

Fasten off, leaving a long tail for sewing.

» Wings

Make 2.

With cream, make a magic circle.

Rnd 1: Work 6 sc in ring.

Rnd 2: *Sc 2 in next sc; rep from * around—12 sts.

Rnd 3: (Sc in next st, 2 sc in following st) 6 times—18 sts.

Rnd 4: (Sc in each of next 2 sts, 2 sc in following st) 6 times—24 sts.

Rnd 5: Sc in each of next 6 sts, (sc in next st, 2 sc in following st) 6 times, sc in each of rem 6 sts—30 sts.

Rnd 6: Sc in each of next 6 sts, (hdc in each of next 2 sts, 2 hdc in next st) 6 times, sc in each of rem 6 sts—36 sts.

Rnd 7: Sc in each of next 16 sts, hdc in next st, 2 dc in next st, ch 3, sl st in base of ch-3 (picot made), 2 dc in next st, hdc in next st, sc in each of rem 16 sts—38 sts.

Fasten off, leaving a long tail for sewing.

» Head and Body

With purple, make a magic circle.

Rnd 1: Work 7 sc in ring.

Rnd 2: *Sc 2 in next sc; rep from * around—14 sts.

Sofie's face and golden crown.

Wing view.

Rnd 3: (Sc in next st, 2 sc in following st) 7 times—21 sts.

Rnd 4: (Sc in each of next 2 sts, 2 sc in following st) 7 times—28 sts.

Rnd 5: (Sc in each of next 3 sts, 2 sc in following st) 7 times—35 sts.

Rnd 6: (Sc in each of next 4 sts, 2 sc in following st) 7 times—42 sts.

Rnd 7: (Sc in each of next 5 sts, 2 sc in following st) 7 times—49 sts.

Rnds 8–22: Sc around.

Rnd 23: Sc in each of next 5 sc, (sc in each of next 3 sts, sc2tog) 7 times, sc in each of rem 9 sts—42 sts.

Rnd 24: Sc in each of next 5 sc, (sc in each of next 2 sts, sc2tog) 7 times, sc in each of rem 9 sts—35 sts.

Rnd 25: Sc in each of next 6 sc, (sc in each of next 2 sts, sc2tog) 5 times, sc in each of rem 9 sts—30 sts.

Rnd 26: Sc in each of next 6 sc, (sc in next st, sc2tog) 6 times, sc in each of rem 6 sts—24 sts.

Rnd 27: Sc in each of next 3 sc, (sc in next st, sc2tog) 6 times, sc in each of rem 3 sts—18 sts.

Sew beak in place on head using yellow gold yarn and referring to photo at right for placement. Attach safety eyes on either side of beak. Stuff as work progresses.

Rnds 28–40: Sc around.

Rnd 41: Sc 2 in each of next 2 sts, sc in next st, sc2tog 5 times, sc in each of next 2 sts, 2 sc in each of next 3 sts—18 sts.

Rnds 42–44: Sc around.

Rnd 45: Sc 2 in each of next 3 sts, sc in each of next 12 sts, 2 sc in each of next 3 sts—24 sts.

Rnd 46: (Sc in next st, 2 sc in following st) 3 times, sc in each of next 12 sts, (sc in next st, 2 sc in following st) 3 times—30 sts.

Rnd 47: (Sc in each of next 2 sts, 2 sc in following st) 3 times, sc in each of next 12 sts, (sc in each of next 2 sts, 2 sc in following st) 3 times—36 sts.

Rnd 48: (Sc in each of next 3 sts, 2 sc in following st) 3 times, sc in each of next 12 sts, (sc in each of next 3 sts, 2 sc in following st) 3 times—42 sts.

Rnd 49: Sc around.

Rnd 50: (Sc in each of next 6 sts, 2 sc in following st) 6 times—48 sts.

Rnd 51: (Sc in each of next 11 sts, 2 sc in following st) 4 times—52 sts.

Rnd 52: (Sc in each of next 12 sts, 2 sc in following st) 4 times—56 sts.

Rnd 53: (Sc in next st, 2 sc in following st) 3 times, sc in each of next 49 sts, 2 sc in last st—60 sts.

Rnds 54–59: Sc around.

Rnd 60: Sc in each of next 25 sts, sc2tog 5 times, sc in each of rem 25 sts—55 sts.

Rnd 61: Sc in each of next 20 sts, (sc in next st, sc2tog) 5 times, sc in each of rem 20 sts—50 sts.

Rnd 62: Sc 2 in next 2 sts, sc in each of next 15 sts, (sc in next st, sc2tog) 5 times, sc in each of next 15 sts, 2 sc in each of next 3 sts—50 sts.

Rnd 63: Sc2tog 2 times, sc in each of next 40 sts, sc2tog 3 times—45 sts.

Rnd 64: Sc in each of next 15 sts, (sc in next st, sc2tog) 5 times, sc in each of rem 15 sts—40 sts.

Sew the beak in place, starting above the decrease section.

Rnd 65: Sc in each of next 10 sts, (sc in each of next 2 sts, sc2tog) 5 times, sc in each of rem 10 sts—35 sts.

Rnd 66: (Sc in each of next 5 sts, sc2tog) 5 times—30 sts.

Rnd 67: (Sc in each of next 3 sts, sc2tog) 6 times—24 sts.

Rnd 68: (Sc in each of next 2 sts, sc2tog) 6 times—18 sts.

Rnd 69: (Sc in next st, sc2tog) 6 times—12 sts.

Rnd 70: Sc in every other st—6 sts.

Fasten off, leaving a long tail for sewing.

»» Assembly

Finish stuffing body. Sew wings to sides of body. Sew crown in place on head. Weave in ends.

» Lila, Littlun's Lamb »

This lamb may use a more complicated stitch—the puff stitch—but take one look at this cuddly lamb and you'll be eager to start crocheting. Using a neutral palette with pink blush on the ears for subtle color makes Lila as sweet as can be.

Skill Level: Intermediate
Finished Size: 10" tall

» Materials

See page 60 for more about yarns.

Yarn:

Light worsted- or DK-weight 4-ply acrylic yarn (3)

140 yds in white for body and wool

100 yds in cream for head, ears, arms, and legs

30 yds in tan for hooves

Hooks and Notions:

US Size F-5 (3.75 mm) crochet hook

2 safety eyes, 15 mm diameter

Stitch marker, fiberfill stuffing, tapestry needle

Cotton swab

Pink powdered blush (cosmetic)

Black embroidery floss

» Head

With cream, make a magic circle (page 61).

Rnd 1: Work 7 sc in ring.

Rnd 2: *Sc 2 in next sc; rep from * around—14 sts.

Rnd 3: (Sc in next st, 2 sc in following st) 7 times—21 sts.

Rnd 4: (Sc in each of next 2 sts, 2 sc in following st) 7 times—28 sts.

Rnd 5: (Sc in each of next 3 sts, 2 sc in following st) 7 times—35 sts.

Rnd 6: (Sc in each of next 4 sts, 2 sc in following st) 7 times—42 sts.

Rnd 7: Sc around.

Rnd 8: (Sc in each of next 5 sts, 2 sc in following st) 7 times—49 sts.

Rnds 9–20: Sc around.

Rnd 21: (Sc in each of next 6 sts, 2 sc in following st) 7 times—56 sts.

Rnd 22: Sc around.

Rnd 23: (Sc in each of next 6 sts, sc2tog) 7 times—49 sts.

Rnd 24: (Sc in each of next 5 sts, sc2tog) 7 times—42 sts.

Rnd 25: (Sc in each of next 4 sts, sc2tog) 7 times—35 sts.

Rnd 26: (Sc in each of next 3 sts, sc2tog) 7 times—28 sts.

Rnd 27: (Sc in each of next 5 sts, sc2tog) 4 times—24 sts.

Fasten off, leaving a long tail for sewing.

» Top Head Wool

Count puff (page 62) as 1 st, and ch 1 at end of puff as a second st throughout. On subsequent rnds, work sts into the top of each puff and in each ch 1.

With white, make a magic circle.

Rnd 1: Work 5 sc in ring.

Rnd 2: Puff (page 62) 5 times—10 sts.

Rnd 3: Sc around.

Rnd 4: Puff 10 times—20 sts.

Rnd 5: (Sc in next st, 2 sc in following st) 10 times—30 sts.

Rnd 6: (Puff, sc in next st) 15 times—45 sts.

Fasten off, leaving a long tail for sewing.

» Head Wool

With white, make a magic circle.

Rnd 1: Work 6 sc in ring.

Rnd 2: *Sc 2 in next sc; rep from * around—12 sts.

Rnd 3: (Sc in next st, 2 sc in following st) 6 times—18 sts.

Wool at the top of Lila's head.

Rnd 4: Sc 2 in each of next 2 sts, sc in each of next 5 sts, 2 sc in each of next 3 sts, sc in each of next 7 sts, 2 sc in last st—24 sts.

Rnd 5: (Sc in next st, 2 sc in following st) 2 times, sc in each of next 5 sts, (sc in next st, 2 sc in following st) 3 times, sc in each of next 8 sts, 2 sc in last st—30 sts.

Rnd 6: (Sc in each of next 4 sts, 2 sc in following st) 6 times—36 sts.

Rnd 7: (Sc in each of next 5 sts, 2 sc in following st) 6 times—42 sts.

Rnd 8: (Sc in each of next 5 sts, 2 sc in following st) 7 times—49 sts.

Rnd 9: (Sc in each of next 6 sts, 2 sc in following st) 7 times—56 sts.

Rnds 10–22: Sc around.

Rnd 23: Through front loops only, sc in each of next 4 sts, ([2 dc in next st] twice, dc, [2 dc in next st] twice, sl st) 7 times, sc in each of rem 10 sts—84 sts.

Fasten off, leaving a long tail for sewing.

Ears

Make 2.

With cream, make a magic circle.

Rnd 1: Work 6 sc in ring.

Rnd 2: *Sc 2 in next sc; rep from * around—12 sts.

Rnd 3: (Sc in next st, 2 sc in following st) 6 times—18 sts.

Rnds 4–6: Sc around.

Rnd 7: (Sc in each of next 4 sts, sc2tog) 3 times—15 sts.

Rnd 8: Sc around.

Rnd 9: (Sc in each of next 3 sts, sc2tog) 3 times—12 sts.

Rnd 10: Sc around.

Rnd 11: (Sc in each of next 2 sts, sc2tog) 3 times—9 sts.

Rnd 12: Sc around.

Fasten off, leaving a long tail for sewing.

Arms

Make 2.

With cream, make a magic circle.

Rnd 1: Work 6 sc in ring.

Rnd 2: *Sc 2 in next sc; rep from * around—12 sts.

Rnd 3: (Sc in each of next 3 sts, 2 sc in following st) 3 times—15 sts.

Rnds 4–6: Sc around.

Rnd 7: (Sc in each of next 3 sts, sc2tog) 3 times—12 sts.

Rnds 8–11: Sc around.

Rnd 12: (Sc in each of next 2 sts, sc2tog) 3 times—9 sts.

Rnds 13–15: Sc around.

Stuff.

Rnd 16: With white, (puff, sc in next st) 4 times, sl st in last st.

Fasten off, leaving a long tail for sewing.

Legs

Make 2.

With tan, make a magic circle.

Rnd 1: Work 6 sc in ring.

Rnd 2: *Sc 2 in next sc; rep from * around—12 sts.

Rnd 3: (Sc in next st, 2 sc in following st) 6 times—18 sts.

Rnd 4: (Sc in each of next 2 sts, 2 sc in following st) 6 times—24 sts.

Rnd 5: Sc in each of next 9 sts, sc2tog 3 times, sc in each of rem 9 sts—21 sts.

Rnd 6: Sc in each of next 6 sts, sc2tog 5 times, sc in each of rem 5 sts—16 sts.

Rnd 7: Sc around.

Rnd 8: With cream, sc around.

Stuff firmly up to this round only.

Rnd 9: (Sc in each of next 2 sts, sc2tog) 4 times—12 sts.

Rnds 10 and 11: Sc around.

Rnd 12: (Sc in each of next 2 sts, sc2tog) 3 times—9 sts.

Rnds 13–16: Sc around.

Fasten off, leaving a long tail for sewing.

Body

With white, make a magic circle.

Count puff as one st, and ch 1 at end of puff as a second st throughout. On subsequent rnds, work sts into the top of each puff and in each ch 1.

Rnd 1: Work 6 sc in ring.

Rnd 2: Puff 6 times—12 sts.

Rnd 3: (Sc in next st, 2 sc in following st) 6 times—18 sts.

Rnd 4: Puff 18 times—36 sts.

Rnd 5: (Sc in each of next 8 sts, 2 sc in following st) 4 times—40 sts.

Rnd 6: (Puff, sc in next st) 20 times—60 sts.

Rnd 7: (Sc in next st, sc2tog) 20 times—40 sts.

Rnd 8: (Puff, sc in next st, puff, sc2tog) 8 times—48 sts.

Rnd 9: (Sc in next st, sc2tog) 16 times—32 sts.

Rnd 10: (Puff, sc in next st) 16 times—48 sts.

Rnd 11: (Sc, sc2tog) 16 times—32 sts.

Rnd 12: (Puff, sc2tog) 10 times, puff, sc in last st—33 sts.

Rnd 13: (Sc in next st, sc2tog) 11 times—22 sts.

Rnd 14: Puff, sc in next st, (puff, sc2tog) 6 times, puff, sc in last st—24 sts.

Rnd 15: (Puff, sc2tog) 8 times—24 sts.

Rnd 16: (Sc in each of next 2 sts, sc2tog) 6 times—18 sts.

Fasten off, leaving a long tail for sewing.

Assembly

Sew top head wool to head wool. Fold end of ears in half, and add a bit of blush to inside of ear using a cotton swab. Sew ears in place on top head wool.

Attach safety eyes between rnds 19 and 20 with approx 12 sts in between. With embroidery floss, embroider a "Y" shape between eyes as shown. Stuff head firmly. Sew head wool to head. Sew feet to body. Stuff arms firmly and sew to body. Stuff body firmly. Sew head in place. Weave in ends.

» Mia Bunny »

A few years back, I learned about a game called "Chubby Bunny," and that phrase inspired the shape of little Mia. Her simple egg-shaped figure is given a personality through her lively green ears, scarf, and cute little tush.

Huggable Amigurumi

Skill Level: Easy
Finished Size: 9¼" tall

Materials

See page 60 for more about yarns.

Yarn:
Light worsted- or DK-weight 4-ply acrylic yarn
160 yds in white for arms, legs, head, and body
60 yds in green for ears, tail, and scarf

Hooks and Notions:
US Size F-5 (3.75 mm) crochet hook
2 buttons, 20 mm diameter, for eyes
Stitch marker, fiberfill stuffing, tapestry needle

Ears

Make 2.

With green, make a magic circle (page 61).

Rnd 1: Work 6 sc in ring.

Rnd 2: *Sc 2 in next sc; rep from * around—12 sts.

Rnd 3: (Sc in next st, 2 sc in following st) 6 times—18 sts.

Rnd 4: (Sc in each of next 2 sts, 2 sc in following st) 6 times—24 sts.

Rnd 5: (Sc in each of next 3 sts, 2 sc in following st) 6 times—30 sts.

Rnds 6–12: Sc around.

Rnd 13: (Sc in each of next 3 sts, sc2tog) 6 times—24 sts.

Rnds 14–18: Sc around.

Rnd 19: (Sc in each of next 2 sts, sc2tog) 6 times—18 sts.

Rnds 20–22: Sc around.

Fasten off, leaving a long tail for sewing.

Arms

Make 2.

With white, make a magic circle.

Rnd 1: Work 6 sc in ring.

Rnd 2: *Sc 2 in next sc; rep from * around—12 sts.

Rnd 3: (Sc in next st, 2 sc in following st) 6 times—18 sts.

Rnds 4–9: Sc around.

Fasten off, leaving a long tail for sewing.

Legs

Make 2.

With white, make a magic circle.

Rnd 1: Work 5 sc in ring.

Rnd 2: *Sc 2 in next sc; rep from * around—10 sts.

Rnd 3: (Sc in next st, 2 sc in following st) 5 times—15 sts.

Rnd 4: (Sc in each of next 2 sts, 2 sc in following st) 5 times—20 sts.

Rnd 5: (Sc in each of next 3 sts, 2 sc in following st) 5 times—25 sts.

Rnd 6: (Sc in each of next 4 sts, 2 sc in following st) 5 times—30 sts.

Rnd 7: Sc around.

Rnd 8: Sc in each of next 12 sts, sc2tog 3 times, sc in each of rem 12 sts—27 sts.

Rnd 9: Sc in each of next 10 sts, sc2tog 3 times, sc in each of rem 11 sts—24 sts.

Leave the ears unstuffed so they'll be flexible.

Stuff the tail before attaching.

Rnd 10: Sc in each of next 9 sts, sc2tog 3 times, sc in each of rem 9 sts—21 sts.

Rnd 11: Sc in each of next 5 sts, sc2tog 6 times, sc in each of rem 4 sts—15 sts.

Rnds 12–15: Sc around.

Fasten off, leaving a long tail for sewing.

» Tail

With green, make a magic circle.

Rnd 1: Work 6 sc in ring.

Rnd 2: *Sc 2 in next sc; rep from * around—12 sts.

Rnd 3: (Sc in next st, 2 sc in following st) 6 times—18 sts.

Rnd 4: (Sc in each of next 2 sts, 2 sc in following st) 6 times—24 sts.

Rnds 5–7: Sc around.

Rnd 8: (Sc in each of next 2 sts, sc2tog) 6 times—18 sts.

Rnd 9: (Sc in next st, sc2tog) 6 times—12 sts.

Fasten off, leaving a long tail for sewing.

» Scarf

With green, ch 88.

Row 1: Hdc in 3rd ch from hook and each ch across.

Fasten off.

» Head and Body

With white, make a magic circle.

Rnd 1: Work 6 sc in ring.

Rnd 2: *Sc 2 in next sc; rep from * around—12 sts.

Rnd 3: (Sc in next st, 2 sc in following st) 6 times—18 sts.

Rnd 4: (Sc in each of next 2 sts, 2 sc in following st) 6 times—24 sts.

Rnd 5: (Sc in each of next 3 sts, 2 sc in following st) 6 times—30 sts.

Rnd 6: (Sc in each of next 4 sts, 2 sc in following st) 6 times—36 sts.

Rnd 7: Sc around.

Rnd 8: (Sc in each of next 5 sts, 2 sc in following st) 6 times—42 sts.

Rnd 9: (Sc in each of next 6 sts, 2 sc in following st) 6 times—48 sts.

Rnd 10: (Sc in each of next 7 sts, 2 sc in following st) 6 times—54 sts.

Rnd 11: (Sc in each of next 8 sts, 2 sc in following st) 6 times—60 sts.

Rnd 12: (Sc in each of next 9 sts, 2 sc in following st) 6 times—66 sts.

Sew ears to top of head, starting at rnd 3.

Rnds 13–32: Sc around.

Sew eyes between rnds 16 and 20, leaving 9 sts in between. With green, embroider a small "X," 2 sts tall and 2 sts wide, between them.

Rnd 33: (Sc in each of next 10 sts, 2 sc in following st) 6 times—72 sts.

Rnds 34–36: Sc around.

Rnd 37: (Sc in each of next 4 sts, sc2tog) 12 times—60 sts.

Rnd 38: (Sc in each of next 8 sts, sc2tog) 6 times—54 sts.

Rnd 39: (Sc in each of next 7 sts, sc2tog) 6 times—48 sts.

Rnd 40: (Sc in each of next 6 sts, sc2tog) 6 times—42 sts.

Rnd 41: (Sc in each of next 5 sts, sc2tog) 6 times—36 sts.

Rnd 42: (Sc in each of next 4 sts, sc2tog) 6 times—30 sts.

Rnd 43: (Sc in each of next 3 sts, sc2tog) 6 times—24 sts.

Stuff firmly.

Wrap the scarf around Mia's neck.

Rnd 44: (Sc in each of next 2 sts, sc2tog) 6 times—18 sts.

Rnd 45: (Sc in next st, sc2tog) 6 times—12 sts.

Rnd 46: Sc in every other st—6 sts.

Fasten off, leaving a long tail for sewing.

» Assembly

Stuff tail, arms, and legs firmly. Sew arms to body, 3 rnds below eyes. Sew tail in place. Sew legs in place as shown. Wrap scarf around neck and sew in place. Weave in ends.

» Connor Frog »

Jazzy Connor's pattern is all about bright colors and unconventional shapes. Made with simple techniques, the different parts combine to create a perfect little frog for playtime. Sparks of color in his accessories add extra pizzazz.

Connor Frog

Skill Level: Easy
Finished Size: 9½" tall

>> Materials

See page 60 for more about yarns.

Yarn:
Light worsted- or DK-weight 4-ply acrylic yarn (3)
120 yds in apple green for head, body, arms, and legs
30 yds in yellow for hat and bow
2 yds in white for eyes
1 yd in brown for trim

Hooks and Notions:
US Size F-5 (3.75 mm) crochet hook
Stitch marker, fiberfill stuffing, tapestry needle

>> Hat

With yellow, make a magic circle (page 61).

Rnd 1: Work 6 sc in ring.
Rnd 2: *Sc 2 in next sc; rep from * around—12 sts.
Rnd 3: (Sc in next st, 2 sc in following st) 6 times—18 sts.
Rnd 4: Through back loops only, sc around.
Rnds 5–8: Sc around.
Rnd 9: Through front loops only, (hdc in next st, 2 hdc in next st) 9 times—27 sts.
Rnd 10: (Sc in each of next 2 sts, 2 sc in following st) 9 times—36 sts.

Fasten off, leaving a long tail for sewing.

>> Front of Eyes

Make 2.

With brown, make a magic circle.

Rnd 1: Work 5 sc in ring.
Rnd 2: With white, *2 sc in next sc; rep from * around—10 sts.
Rnd 3: (Sc in next st, 2 sc in following st) 5 times—15 sts.
Rnd 4: (Sc in each of next 2 sts, 2 sc in following st) 5 times—20 sts.

Fasten off.

>> Back of Eyes

Make 2.

With white, make a magic circle.

Rnd 1: Work 5 sc in ring.
Rnd 2: *Sc 2 in next sc; rep from * around—10 sts.
Rnd 3: (Sc in next st, 2 sc in following st) 5 times—15 sts.
Rnd 4: (Sc in each of next 2 sts, 2 sc in following st) 5 times—20 sts.

Fasten off, leaving a long tail for sewing.

>> Head

With apple green, make a magic circle.

Rnd 1: Work 7 sc in ring.
Rnd 2: *Sc 2 in next sc; rep from * around—14 sts.
Rnd 3: (Sc in next st, 2 sc in following st) 7 times—21 sts.
Rnd 4: (Sc in each of next 2 sts, 2 sc in following st) 7 times—28 sts.
Rnd 5: (Sc in each of next 3 sts, 2 sc in following st) 7 times—35 sts.
Rnds 6–8: Sc around.
Rnd 9: (Sc in each of next 4 sts, 2 sc in following st) 7 times—42 sts.
Rnd 10: (Sc in each of next 5 sts, 2 sc in following st) 7 times—49 sts.

Connor's dapper hat.

Rnd 11: (Sc in each of next 6 sts, 2 sc in following st) 7 times—56 sts.
Rnds 12–21: Sc around.
Rnd 22: (Sc in each of next 6 sts, sc2tog) 7 times—49 sts.
Rnd 23: (Sc in each of next 5 sts, sc2tog) 7 times—42 sts.
Rnd 24: (Sc in each of next 4 sts, sc2tog) 7 times—35 sts.
Rnd 25: (Sc in each of next 3 sts, sc2tog) 7 times—28 sts.
Rnd 26: (Sc in each of next 2 sts, sc2tog) 7 times—21 sts.
Rnd 27: (Sc in next st, sc2tog) 7 times—14 sts.

Fasten off.

>> Bow Tie

With yellow, ch 15.

Row 1: Hdc in 3rd ch from hook and in each ch across, turn—13 sts.
Rows 2 and 3: Ch 2, hdc across, turn—13 sts.
Row 4: Ch 2, hdc across.

Fasten off.

Huggable Amigurumi

Side view of limb alignment.

›› Body

With apple green, make a magic circle.

Rnd 1: Work 6 sc in ring.

Rnd 2: *Sc 2 in next sc; rep from * around—12 sts.

Rnd 3: (Sc in next st, 2 sc in following st) 6 times—18 sts.

Rnd 4: (Sc in each of next 2 sts, 2 sc in following st) 6 times—24 sts.

Rnd 5: (Sc in each of next 3 sts, 2 sc in following st) 6 times—30 sts.

Rnd 6: (Sc in each of next 4 sts, 2 sc in following st) 6 times—36 sts.

Rnd 7: (Sc in each of next 5 sts, 2 sc in following st) 6 times—42 sts.

Rnd 8: (Sc in each of next 6 sts, 2 sc in following st) 6 times—48 sts.

Rnd 9: (Sc in each of next 7 sts, 2 sc in following st) 6 times—54 sts.

Rnds 10–14: Sc around.

Rnd 15: (Sc in each of next 7 sts, sc2tog) 6 times—48 sts.

Rnds 16–18: Sc around.

Rnd 19: (Sc in each of next 6 sts, sc2tog) 6 times—42 sts.

Rnds 20–22: Sc around.

Rnd 23: (Sc in each of next 5 sts, sc2tog) 6 times—36 sts.

Rnds 24–26: Sc around.

Rnd 27: (Sc in each of next 4 sts, sc2tog) 6 times—30 sts.

Rnds 28 and 29: Sc around.

Rnd 30: (Sc in each of next 3 sts, sc2tog) 6 times—24 sts.

Rnd 31: Sc around.

Rnd 32: (Sc in each of next 2 sts, sc2tog) 6 times—18 sts.

Rnd 33: Sc around.

Fasten off, leaving a long tail for sewing.

›› Arms

Make 2.

With apple green, make a magic circle.

Rnd 1: Work 6 sc in ring.

Rnd 2: *Sc 2 in next sc; rep from * around—12 sts.

Rnd 3: (Sc in next st, 2 sc in following st) 6 times—18 sts.

Rnds 4–11: Sc around.

Rnd 12: (Sc in next st, sc2tog) 6 times—12 sts.

Rnds 13–32: Sc around.

Fasten off, leaving a long tail for sewing.

›› Legs

Make 2.

With apple green, make a magic circle.

Rnd 1: Work 6 sc in ring.

Rnd 2: *Sc 2 in next sc; rep from * around—12 sts.

Rnd 3: (Sc in next st, 2 sc in following st) 6 times—18 sts.

Rnd 4: (Sc in each of next 2 sts, 2 sc in following st) 6 times—24 sts.

Rnd 5: (Sc in each of next 3 sts, 2 sc in following st) 6 times—30 sts.

Rnd 6: Sc in each of first 9 sts, sc2tog 6 times, sc in each of rem 9 sts—24 sts.

Rnd 7: Sc in each of next 6 sts, sc2tog 6 times, sc in each of rem 6 sts—18 sts.

Rnd 8: Sc in each of next 6 sts, sc2tog 3 times, sc in each of rem 6 sts—15 sts.

Rnds 9–13: Sc around.

Rnd 14: (Sc in each of next 3 sts, sc2tog) 3 times—12 sts.

Rnds 15 and 16: Sc around.

Rnd 17: (Sc in each of next 2 sts, sc2tog) 3 times—9 sts.

Rnd 18: Sc around.

Fasten off, leaving a long tail for sewing.

›› Assembly

Sew hat to head. Sew backs of eyes to fronts, lightly stuffing if desired. Sew eyes directly beside hat on each side of head. With brown, embroider a wide "V" in center of head for smile. Stuff head firmly. Wrap white yarn tightly around center of bow tie to shape it. Sew in place. Stuff arms lightly; do not stuff legs. Sew arms and legs to body. Stuff body firmly. Sew head in place on body. Weave in ends.

» Brian Turtle »

What a cute little turtle! Brian's bright-blue shell gives him a very beachy feel, or you might try dark green or brown for a woodland look. His pattern is easy to learn, so you'll want to make more than one!

Huggable Amigurumi

Skill Level: Beginner
Finished Size: 9½" long

» Materials

See page 60 for more about yarns.

Yarn:

Light worsted- or DK-weight 4-ply acrylic yarn (3)

90 yds in apple green for head, arms, and legs

90 yds in blue for shell

Hooks and Notions:

US Size F-5 (3.75 mm) crochet hook

2 buttons, 20 mm diameter, for eyes

Stitch marker, fiberfill stuffing, tapestry needle

» Head

With apple green, make a magic circle (page 61).

Rnd 1: Work 6 sc in ring.

Rnd 2: *Sc 2 in next sc; rep from * around—12 sts.

Rnd 3: (Sc in next st, 2 sc in following st) 6 times—18 sts.

Rnd 4: (Sc in each of next 2 sts, 2 sc in following st) 6 times—24 sts.

Rnd 5: (Sc in each of next 3 sts, 2 sc in following st) 6 times—30 sts.

Rnd 6: (Sc in each of next 4 sts, 2 sc in following st) 6 times—36 sts.

Rnd 7: (Sc in each of next 5 sts, 2 sc in following st) 6 times—42 sts.

Rnd 8: (Sc in each of next 6 sts, 2 sc in following st) 6 times—48 sts.

Rnds 9–21: Sc around.

Rnd 22: Sc in each of next 22 sts, 2 sc in each of next 4 sts (nose made), sc in each of rem 22 sts—52 sts.

Rnd 23: Sc in each of next 22 sts, sc2tog 4 times, sc in each of rem 22 sts—48 sts.

Rnd 24: (Sc in each of next 6 sts, sc2tog) 6 times—42 sts.

Rnd 25: (Sc in each of next 5 sts, sc2tog) 6 times—36 sts.

Sew eyes in place on head. Stuff firmly.

Rnd 26: (Sc in each of next 4 sts, sc2tog) 6 times—30 sts.

Rnd 27: (Sc in each of next 3 sts, sc2tog) 6 times—24 sts.

Rnd 28: (Sc in each of next 2 sts, sc2tog) 6 times—18 sts.

Rnd 29: (Sc in next st, sc2tog) 6 times—12 sts.

Rnd 30: Sc in every other st—6 sts.

Fasten off.

Stuff head. Weave in ends, pulling yarn tail through back of head and leaving it long for sewing.

» Shell

With blue, ch 7.

Rnd 1: Sc in 2nd ch from hook and in each of next 4 sts, 2 sc in following st. Turn foundation ch, sc in each of first 5 ch, 2 sc in last ch—14 sts.

Rnd 2: (Sc in next st, 2 sc in following st) 7 times—21 sts.

Top-down view of Brian's shell.

Rnd 3: (Sc in each of next 2 sts, 2 sc in following st) 7 times—28 sts.

Rnd 4: (Sc in each of next 3 sts, 2 sc in following st) 7 times—35 sts.

Rnd 5: (Sc in each of next 4 sts, 2 sc in following st) 7 times—42 sts.

Rnd 6: (Sc in each of next 5 sts, 2 sc in following st) 7 times—49 sts.

Rnd 7: (Sc in each of next 6 sts, 2 sc in following st) 7 times—56 sts.

Rnd 8: (Sc in each of next 7 sts, 2 sc in following st) 7 times—63 sts.

Rnd 9: Hdc around.

Rnd 10: (Sc in each of next 8 sts, 2 sc in following st) 7 times—70 sts.

Rnds 11–16: Sc around.

Rnd 17: Through front loops only, (hdc in each of next 4 sts, 2 hdc in following st) 14 times—84 sts. Through back loops only of same rnd, (sc in each of next 2 sts, sc2tog) 21 times—63 sts.

Rnd 18: (Sc in each of next 7 sts, sc2tog) 7 times—56 sts.

Rnd 19: (Sc in each of next 6 sts, sc2tog) 7 times—49 sts.

Rnd 20: (Sc in each of next 5 sts, sc2tog) 7 times—42 sts.

Rnd 21: (Sc in each of next 4 sts, sc2tog) 7 times—35 sts.

Rnd 22: (Sc in each of next 3 sts, sc2tog) 7 times—28 sts.

Rnd 23: (Sc in each of next 2 sts, sc2tog) 7 times—21 sts.

Rnd 24: (Sc in next st, sc2tog) 7 times—14 sts.

Rnd 25: Sc in every other st—7 sts.

Fasten off.

Stuff firmly. Weave in ends.

» Arms

Make 2.

With apple green, make a magic circle.

Rnd 1: Work 6 sc in ring.

Rnd 2: *Sc 2 in next sc; rep from * around—12 sts.

Rnd 3: (Sc in each of next 3 sts, 2 sc in following st) 3 times—15 sts.

Rnds 4–12: Sc around.

Fasten off, leaving a long tail for sewing.

» Legs

Make 2.

With apple green, make a magic circle.

Rnd 1: Work 6 sc in ring.

Rnd 2: *Sc 2 in next sc; rep from * around—12 sts.

Rnd 3: Sc in each of next 3 sts, 2 sc in each of next 6 sts, sc in each of rem 3 sts—18 sts.

Rnd 4: Sc in each of next 3 sts, (sc in next st, 2 sc in following st) 6 times, sc in each of rem 3 sts—24 sts.

Rnd 5: Sc around.

Rnd 6: Sc in each of next 3 sts, (sc in next st, sc2tog) 6 times, sc in each of rem 3 sts—18 sts.

Rnd 7: Sc in each of next 3 sts, sc2tog 6 times, sc in each of rem 3 sts—12 sts.

Rnds 8–15: Sc around.

Fasten off, leaving a long tail for sewing.

» Assembly

Sew arms and legs to bottom of shell. Sew head to shell using yarn tail on head.

Leg and arm placement.

Eye placement.

» Elliott Giraffe »

Elliott is one of the thinner amigurumi in this book, but that doesn't mean he's not as fun to hug and play with! With his bright-blue spots, cream muzzle, and yellow body, he's one little giraffe ready for fun.

Skill Level: Easy
Finished Size: 10" tall

» Materials

See page 60 for more about yarns.

Yarn:

Light worsted- or DK-weight 4-ply acrylic yarn (3)

90 yds in yellow for ears, head, body, and legs

45 yds in blue for spots, mane, horns, and tail

5 yds in cream for muzzle

3 yds in chocolate brown for trim

Hooks and Notions:

US Size F-5 (3.75 mm) crochet hook

2 safety eyes, 15 mm diameter

Stitch marker, fiberfill stuffing, tapestry needle

» Horns

Make 2.

With blue, make a magic circle (page 61).

Rnd 1: Work 4 sc in ring.

Rnd 2: *Sc 2 in next sc; rep from * around—8 sts.

Rnds 3–5: Sc around.

Fasten off, leaving a long tail for sewing.

» Ears

Make 2.

With yellow, make a magic circle.

Rnd 1: Work 4 sc in ring.

Rnd 2: *Sc 2 in next sc; rep from * around—8 sts.

Rnd 3: (Sc in next st, 2 sc in following st) 4 times—12 sts.

Rnd 4: (Sc in each of next 2 sts, 2 sc in following st) 4 times—16 sts.

Rnds 5 and 6: Sc around.

Rnd 7: (Sc in each of next 2 sts, sc2tog) 4 times—12 sts.

Rnd 8: Sc around.

Rnd 9: (Sc in next st, sc2tog) 4 times—8 sts.

Fasten off, leaving a long tail for sewing.

» Spots

Make 5 or number desired.

With blue, make a magic circle.

Rnd 1: Work 5 sc in ring.

Rnd 2: *Sc 2 in next sc; rep from * around—10 sts.

Fasten off, leaving a long tail for sewing.

» Mane

With blue, ch 40.

Make 4 hdc in 3rd ch from hook, sl st in next st, *ch 3, sc in 2nd and 3rd ch from hook, sl st in next ch of foundation ch; rep from * to end.

Fasten off, leaving a long tail for sewing.

» Head

With yellow, make a magic circle.

Rnd 1: Work 6 sc in ring.

Rnd 2: *Sc 2 in next sc; rep from * around—12 sts.

Rnd 3: (Sc in next st, 2 sc in following st) 6 times—18 sts.

Rnd 4: (Sc in each of next 2 sts, 2 sc in following st) 6 times—24 sts.

Rnd 5: (Sc in each of next 3 sts, 2 sc in following st) 6 times—30 sts.

Rnd 6: (Sc in each of next 5 sts, 2 sc in following st) 5 times—35 sts.

Elliott's mane is crocheted separately and attached during finishing.

Rnd 7: (Sc in each of next 6 sts, 2 sc in following st) 5 times—40 sts.

Rnds 8–16: Sc around.

Rnd 17: With cream, (sc in each of next 7 sts, 2 sc in following st) 5 times—45 sts.

Rnd 18: Sc around.

Rnd 19: (Sc in each of next 7 sts, sc2tog) 5 times—40 sts.

Rnd 20: (Sc in each of next 3 sts, sc2tog) 8 times—32 sts.

Rnd 21: (Sc in each of next 2 sts, sc2tog) 8 times—24 sts.

Rnd 22: (Sc in each of next 2 sts, sc2tog) 6 times—18 sts.

Rnd 23: (Sc in next st, sc2tog) 6 times—12 sts.

Rnds 24–32: With yellow, sc around.

Fasten off, leaving a long tail for sewing.

Huggable Amigurumi

Embroidered nose.

Horn and mane placement.

» Body

With yellow, make a magic circle.

Rnd 1: Work 6 sc in ring.

Rnd 2: *Sc 2 in next sc; rep from * around—12 sts.

Rnd 3: Sc in each of next 2 sts, 2 sc in each of next 6 sts, sc in each of rem 4 sts—18 sts.

Rnd 4: Sc in each of next 2 sts, (sc in next st, 2 sc in following st) 6 times, sc in each of rem 4 sts—24 sts.

Rnd 5: Sc in each of next 2 sts, (sc in each of next 2 sts, 2 sc in following st) 6 times, sc in each of rem 4 sts—30 sts.

Rnd 6: Sc in each of next 12 sts, 2 sc in each of next 6 sts, sc in each of rem 12 sts—36 sts.

Rnd 7: Sc in each of next 15 sts, 2 sc in each of next 6 sts, sc in each of rem 15 sts—42 sts.

Rnds 8 and 9: Sc around.

Rnd 10: (Sc in each of next 5 sts, sc2tog) 6 times—36 sts.

Rnds 11–13: Sc around.

Rnd 14: (Sc in each of next 4 sts, sc2tog) 6 times—30 sts.

Rnd 15: (Sc in each of next 3 sts, sc2tog) 6 times—24 sts.

Rnd 16: (Sc in each of next 2 sts, sc2tog) 6 times—18 sts.

Rnd 17: (Sc in next st, sc2tog) 6 times—12 sts.

Rnd 18: (Sc in next st, sc2tog) 4 times—8 sts.

Rnd 19: (Sc in next 2 sts, sc2tog) 2 times—6 sts.

Fasten off, leaving a long tail for sewing.

» Legs

Make 4.

With chocolate brown, make a magic circle.

Rnd 1: Work 4 sc in ring.

Rnd 2: *Sc 2 in next sc; rep from * around—8 sts.

Rnds 3 and 4: Sc around.

Rnds 5–14: With yellow, sc around.

Rnd 15: Sc 2 in each of next 2 sts, sc in each of next 6 sts—10 sts.

Fasten off, leaving a long tail for sewing.

» Tail

With blue, ch 10.

Sc 3 in 2nd ch from hook and sl st in every other st across.

Fasten off, leaving a long tail for sewing.

» Assembly

Attach safety eyes just above color change, leaving 10 sts between eyes. With chocolate brown, embroider small "Y" for nose. Sew ears to head.

Sew horns to top of head, leaving room for mane. Sew mane in place, starting with rnd 5 on front of head.

Sew spots in place as desired. Sew tail to body. Firmly stuff head, body, and legs. Sew neck to body. Sew legs in place. Weave in ends.

» Moby Whale »

For little Moby, color and simplicity are what it's all about. A simple shaping technique and double-stranded variegated yarn create that gorgeous mix of blues, yellow, and white you can find in the ocean. Double stranding adds extra cushion too! Shiny beads act as water droplets to top off the look with extra glitter and glam.

Huggable Amigurumi

Skill Level: Easy
Finished Size: 11" long

Materials

See page 60 for more about yarns.

Yarn:

Light worsted- or DK-weight 4-ply acrylic yarn

500 yds in yellow-and-blue variegated for body

10 yds in blue for water spout and fins

Hooks and Notions:

US Size 7 (4.5 mm) crochet hook

US Size E-4 (3.5 mm) crochet hook

2 buttons, 20 mm diameter, for eyes

Stitch marker, fiberfill stuffing, tapestry needle

Round glass beads, in number desired

Embroidery floss, in color to match beads

Water Spout

With blue and smaller hook, make a magic circle (page 61).

Rnd 1: Work 6 sc in ring.

Rnd 2: *Sc 2 in next sc; rep from * around—12 sts.

Rnd 3: Sc around.

Rnd 4: (Ch 5, sc in 2nd ch from hook and in each of next 3 ch, sl st through front loop only of next st) 12 times. Through back loops only of same rnd, (sc in each of next 2 sts, sc2tog) 3 times—9 sts.

Rnds 5–9: Sc around.

Fasten off, leaving a long tail for sewing.

Fins

Make 2.

With blue and smaller hook, make a magic circle.

Rnd 1: Work 6 sc in ring.

Rnd 2: *Sc 2 in next sc; rep from * around—12 sts.

Rnd 3: (Sc in next st, 2 sc in following st) 6 times—18 sts.

Rnd 4: (Sc in each of next 2 sts, 2 sc in following st) 6 times—24 sts.

Rnd 5: Sc in each of next 11 sts, hdc in next st, ch 1, hdc in next st, sc in each of rem 11 sts—24 sts.

Fasten off, leaving a long tail for sewing.

Body

With 2 strands of yellow-and-blue variegated and larger hook, make a magic circle.

Rnd 1: Work 6 sc in ring.

Rnd 2: *Sc 2 in next sc; rep from * around—12 sts.

Rnd 3: (Sc in next st, 2 sc in following st) 6 times—18 sts.

Rnd 4: (Sc in each of next 2 sts, 2 sc in following st) 6 times—24 sts.

Rnd 5: (Sc in each of next 3 sts, 2 sc in following st) 6 times—30 sts.

Rnd 6: (Sc in each of next 4 sts, 2 sc in following st) 6 times—36 sts.

Rnd 7: (Sc in each of next 5 sts, 2 sc in following st) 6 times—42 sts.

Rnd 8: (Sc in each of next 6 sts, 2 sc in following st) 6 times—48 sts.

Fin stitched to Moby's side.

Top view of water spout.

Rnd 9: (Sc in each of next 7 sts, 2 sc in following st) 6 times—54 sts.

Rnd 10: (Sc in each of next 8 sts, 2 sc in following st) 6 times—60 sts.

Rnd 11: (Sc in each of next 9 sts, 2 sc in following st) 6 times—66 sts.

Rnds 12–23: Sc around.

Rnd 24: Sc in each of next 27 sts, sc2tog 6 times, sc in each of rem 27 sts—60 sts.

Rnds 25–27: Sc around.

Rnd 28: Sc in each of next 21 sts, (sc in next st, sc2tog in next st) 6 times, sc in each of rem 21 sts—54 sts.

Rnds 29–31: Sc around.

Rnd 32: Sc in each of next 18 sts, (sc in next st, sc2tog in next st) 6 times, sc in each of rem 18 sts—48 sts. Begin stuffing.

Rnd 33: Sc around.

Rnd 34: Sc in each of next 6 sts, (sc in next st, sc2tog in next st) 12 times, sc in each of rem 6 sts—36 sts.

Rnds 35 and 36: Sc around.

Rnd 37: (Sc in next st, sc2tog) 3 times, sc in each of next 18 sts, (sc in next st, sc2tog) 3 times—30 sts.

Rnds 38 and 39: Sc around.

Rnd 40: (Sc in next st, sc2tog) 3 times, (sc in next st, 2 sc in following st) 6 times, (sc in next st, sc2tog) 3 times—30 sts.

Rnds 41 and 42: Sc around.

Rnd 43: Rep rnd 40.

Rnds 44 and 45: Sc around.

Rnd 46: Rep rnd 40.

Rnds 47 and 48: Sc around.

Rnd 49: Sc in each of next 7 sts, (sc in each of next 2 sts, 2 sc in following st) 5 times, sc in each of remaining 8 sts—35 sts.

Rnds 50 and 51: Sc around.

Rnd 52: (Sc in each of next 5 sts, sc2tog) 5 times—30 sts.

Rnd 53: (Sc in each of next 3 sts, sc2tog) 6 times—24 sts.

Rnd 54: (Sl st, sc, 2 hdc, hdc, dc, 2 dc, 2 dc, dc, hdc, 2 hdc, sc, sl st) 2 times—32 sts.

Rnds 55 and 56: (Sl st, sc, hdc in each of next 3 sts, dc in each of next 6 sts, hdc in each of next 3 st, sc, sl st) 2 times—32 sts.

Fasten off, leaving a long tail for sewing.

Beads sewn to the spout add the look of water droplets.

》Assembly

Sew beads to lower edge of water spout. Stuff spout firmly.

Sew eyes, fins, and water spout in place. Stuff rest of body firmly. Flatten tail and sew tog.

》TIPS AND TRICKS

Over my past few years of making amigurumi, I've stumbled onto some cool tips and tricks that will immediately make your amigurumi stand out!

- If you want your stitches to look like Xs (like mine), wrap the yarn around the hook from the bottom up (opposite of the usual way) after inserting your hook through the stitch. Complete as normal.

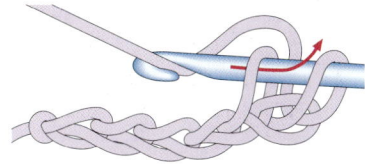

- Hate overstuffed amigurumi? Shape your amigurumi as you would a clay figure and remove any excess stuffing. This neat and dandy trick makes for perfectly stuffed amigurumi every time!

- Want your amigurumi to double as a rattle? Fill a small plastic case halfway with little beads. Tape it securely and stuff it together with the fiberfill stuffing.

- If you want to give your amigurumi a little extra pizzazz, use a cotton swab to brush powdered blush (even shavings from a pink/red colored pencil will do) onto your ami.

- Want your toys to be bendable? Cut lengths of coated wire or pipe cleaners to fit and insert into legs, tail—any part you'd like—then stuff.

» Monty Monkey »

Monty's vibrant personality is matched perfectly by his bright blue fur! Although some assembly is required with Monty, the simplicity of the pattern makes up for it. From his cute muzzle to unique button eyes, Monty's the perfect monkey to hug at night.

Skill Level: Easy
Finished Size: 13½" tall

>> Materials

See page 60 for more about yarns.

Yarn:

Light worsted- or DK-weight 4-ply acrylic yarn (3)

200 yds in blue for head, ears, body, arms, legs, and tail

65 yds in cream for face, tummy, and trim

1 yd in gray for smile

Hooks and Notions:

US Size F-5 (3.75 mm) crochet hook

2 buttons, 15 mm diameter, for eyes

Stitch marker, fiberfill stuffing, tapestry needle

>> Face

With cream, ch 7.

Rnd 1: Sc in 2nd ch from hook and in each of next 4 ch, 2 sc in last st. Turn foundation ch. On opposite side of foundation ch, sc in each of next 5 ch, 2 sc in last ch—14 sts.

Rnd 2: (Sc in next st, 2 sc in following st) 7 times—21 sts.

Rnd 3: (Sc in each of next 2 sts, 2 sc in following st) 7 times—28 sts.

Rnd 4: (Sc in each of next 3 sts, 2 sc in following st) 7 times—35 sts.

Rnd 5: (Sc in each of next 4 sts, 2 sc in following st) 7 times—42 sts.

Rnds 6–9: Sc around.

Rnd 10: (Sc in each of next 5 sts, sc2tog) 6 times—36 sts.

Begin working back and forth in rows.

Row 1: Through front loops only, sc in each of next 14 sts, ch 1, turn—14 sts.

Rows 2–6: Sc in each st across, ch 1, turn.

Row 7: Sc2tog, sc in each of next 10 sts, sc2tog, ch 1, turn—12 sts.

Row 8: Sc in each of next 2 sts, hdc in each of next 2 sts, dc in next st, (2 dc in next st) 2 times, dc in next st, hdc in each of next 2 sts, sc in each of rem 2 sts—14 sts.

Fasten off, leaving a long tail for sewing.

>> Head

With blue, make a magic circle (page 61).

Rnd 1: Work 6 sc in ring.

Rnd 2: *Sc 2 in next sc; rep from * around—12 sts.

Rnd 3: (Sc in next st, 2 sc in following st) 6 times—18 sts.

Rnd 4: (Sc in each of next 2 sts, 2 sc in following st) 6 times—24 sts.

Rnd 5: (Sc in each of next 3 sts, 2 sc in following st) 6 times—30 sts.

Rnd 6: (Sc in each of next 4 sts, 2 sc in following st) 6 times—36 sts.

Rnd 7: (Sc in each of next 5 sts, 2 sc in following st) 6 times—42 sts.

Rnd 8: (Sc in each of next 6 sts, 2 sc in following st) 6 times—48 sts.

Rnds 9–23: Sc around.

Rnd 24: (Sc in each of next 6 sts, sc2tog) 6 times—42 sts.

Rnd 25: (Sc in each of next 5 sts, sc2tog) 6 times—36 sts.

Rnd 26: (Sc in each of next 4 sts, sc2tog) 6 times—30 sts.

Rnd 27: (Sc in each of next 3 sts, sc2tog) 6 times—24 sts.

Rnd 28: (Sc in each of next 2 sts, sc2tog) 6 times—18 sts.

Fasten off.

>> Inner Ears

Make 2.

With cream, make a magic circle.

Rnd 1: Work 7 sc in ring.

Rnd 2: *Sc 2 in next sc; rep from * around—14 sts.

Rnd 3: (Sc in next st, 2 sc in following st) 7 times—21 sts.

Fasten off, leaving a long tail for sewing.

>> Outer Ears

Make 2.

With blue, make a magic circle.

Rnd 1: Work 8 sc in ring.

Rnd 2: *Sc 2 in next sc; rep from * around—16 sts.

Rnd 3: (Sc in next st, 2 sc in following st) 8 times—24 sts.

Rnd 4: Sc around.

Fasten off, leaving a long tail for sewing.

>> Body

With blue, make a magic circle.

Rnd 1: Work 7 sc in ring.

Rnd 2: *Sc 2 in next sc; rep from * around—14 sts.

Rnd 3: (Sc in next st, 2 sc in following st) 7 times—21 sts.

Rnd 4: (Sc in each of next 2 sts, 2 sc in following st) 7 times—28 sts.

Rnd 5: (Sc in each of next 3 sts, 2 sc in following st) 7 times—35 sts.

Rnd 6: (Sc in each of next 4 sts, 2 sc in following st) 7 times—42 sts.

Huggable Amigurumi

Leave the tail unstuffed.

Embroider Monty's mouth.

Rnd 7: (Sc in each of next 5 sts, 2 sc in following st) 7 times—49 sts.

Rnds 8–12: Sc around.

Rnd 13: (Sc in each of next 5 sts, sc2tog) 7 times—42 sts.

Rnds 14–16: Sc around.

Rnd 17: (Sc in each of next 4 sts, sc2tog) 7 times—35 sts.

Rnds 18–21: Sc around.

Rnd 22: (Sc in each of next 5 sts, sc2tog) 5 times—30 sts.

Rnds 23 and 24: Sc around.

Rnd 25: (Sc in each of next 4 sts, sc2tog) 5 times—25 sts.

Rnds 26–28: Sc around.

Rnd 29: (Sc in each of next 3 sts, sc2tog) 5 times—20 sts.

Rnds 30 and 31: Sc around.

Fasten off, leaving a long tail for sewing.

» Tummy

With cream, make a magic circle.

Rnd 1: Work 6 sc in ring.

Rnd 2: *Hdc 2 in next sc; rep from * around—12 sts.

Rnd 3: (Hdc in next st, 2 hdc in next st) 6 times—18 sts.

Rnd 4: (Hdc in each of next 2 sts, 2 hdc in next st) 6 times—24 sts.

Rnd 5: Sc in each of next 9 sts, 2 hdc in each of next 6 sts, sc in each of rem 9 sts—30 sts.

Fasten off, leaving a long tail for sewing.

» Arms

Make 2.

With cream, make a magic circle.

Rnd 1: Work 6 sc in ring.

Rnd 2: *Sc 2 in next sc; rep from * around—12 sts.

Rnd 3: (Sc in next st, 2 sc in following st) 6 times—18 sts.

Rnds 4–7: Sc around.

Rnds 8 and 9: With blue, sc around.

Rnd 10: (Sc in each of next 4 sts, sc2tog) 3 times—15 sts.

Rnds 11–20: Sc around.

Rnd 21: (Sc in next st, sc2tog) 5 times—10 sts.

Rnds 22–28: Sc around.

Fasten off, leaving a long tail for sewing.

» Legs

Make 2.

With cream, make a magic circle.

Rnd 1: Work 6 sc in ring.

Rnd 2: *Sc 2 in next sc; rep from * around—12 sts.

Rnd 3: (Sc in next st, 2 sc in following st) 6 times—18 sts.

Rnd 4: (Sc in each of next 2 sts, 2 sc in following st) 6 times—24 sts.

Rnd 5: (Sc in each of next 3 sts, 2 sc in following st) 6 times—30 sts.

Rnds 6–9: Sc around.

Rnd 10: With blue, sc around.

Rnd 11: (Sc in each of next 3 sts, sc2tog) 6 times—24 sts.

Rnds 12–16: Sc around.

Rnd 17: (Sc in each of next 2 sts, sc2tog) 6 times—18 sts.

Rnds 18–26: Sc around.

Rnd 27: (Sc in next st, sc2tog) 6 times—12 sts.

Rnds 28 and 29: Sc around.

Fasten off, leaving a long tail for sewing.

» Tail

With blue, make a magic circle.

Rnd 1: Work 5 sc in ring.

Rnd 2: *Sc 2 in next sc; rep from * around—10 sts.

Rnds 3–30: Sc around.

Fasten off, leaving a long tail for sewing.

» Assembly

Sew eyes to face, just above where work changes to rows from rounds. With gray and running stitch, embroider mouth as shown at left. Sew face to head. Sew inner and outer ears together. Sew tummy to body. Stuff head, arms, and legs. Sew arms, legs, and tail (unstuffed) in place on body. Sew head to body. Weave in ends.

» Tommy Turkey »

Tommy's quirky personality and trademark black hat make him everybody's beloved turkey friend. His pattern is quick and easy to work up, with fun customizable tail feathers too.

> Huggable Amigurumi

Skill Level: Easy
Finished Size: 9½" tall

Materials

See page 60 for more about yarns.

Yarn:

Light worsted- or DK-weight 4-ply acrylic yarn (3)

60 yds in brown for head and hat band

45 yds in tan for body

40 yds in yellow gold for legs, beak, and feathers

30 yds in red for feathers and snood

25 yds in black for hat

10 yds in orange for feathers

5 yds in moss green for feathers

Hooks and Notions:

US Size F-5 (3.75 mm) crochet hook

2 safety eyes, 14 mm diameter

Stitch marker, fiberfill stuffing, tapestry needle

Beak

With yellow gold, make a magic circle (page 61).

Rnd 1: Work 5 sc in ring.

Rnd 2: *Sc 2 in next sc; rep from * around—10 sts.

Rnd 3: Sc around.

Rnd 4: (Sc in next st, 2 sc in following st) 5 times—15 sts.

Rnd 5: (Sc in each of next 2 sts, 2 sc in following st) 5 times—20 sts.

Fasten off, leaving a long tail for sewing.

Snood

With red, ch 17.

Make 3 hdc in 3rd ch from hook, sl st in next ch, hdc in each of next 4 ch, sc in each of next 5 ch, (dc in next ch, ch 1) 2 times, dc in next ch, sl st in last ch.

Fasten off, leaving a long tail for sewing.

Hat

With black, make a magic circle.

Rnd 1: Work 5 sc in ring.

Rnd 2: *Sc 2 in next sc; rep from * around—10 sts.

Rnd 3: (Sc in next st, 2 sc in following st) 5 times—15 sts.

Rnd 4: (Sc in each of next 2 sts, 2 sc in following st) 5 times—20 sts.

Rnds 5–8: Sc around.

Rnd 9: With brown, (sc in each of next 3 sts, 2 sc in following st) 5 times—25 sts.

Rnd 10: Sc around.

Rnd 11: With black, through front loops only, (sc in each of next 4 sts, 2 sc in following st) 5 times—30 sts.

Rnd 12: (Sc in each of next 4 sts, 2 sc in following st) 6 times—36 sts.

Fasten off, leaving a long tail for sewing.

Head and Body

With brown, make a magic circle.

Rnd 1: Work 6 sc in ring.

Rnd 2: *Sc 2 in next sc; rep from * around—12 sts.

Rnd 3: (Sc in next st, 2 sc in following st) 6 times—18 sts.

Embroider the buckle on the front of the hat.

Rnd 4: (Sc in each of next 2 sts, 2 sc in following st) 6 times—24 sts.

Rnd 5: (Sc in each of next 3 sts, 2 sc in following st) 6 times—30 sts.

Rnd 6: (Sc in each of next 4 sts, 2 sc in following st) 6 times—36 sts.

Rnd 7: (Sc in each of next 8 sts, 2 sc in following st) 4 times—40 sts.

Rnds 8–15: Sc around.

Rnd 16: (Sc in each of next 3 sts, sc2tog) 8 times—32 sts.

Attach safety eyes, leaving room for beak in between.

Rnd 17: (Sc in each of next 2 sts, sc2tog) 8 times—24 sts.

Rnd 18: (Sc in each of next 2 sts, sc2tog) 6 times—18 sts.

Rnd 19: (Sc in next st, sc2tog) 6 times—12 sts.

Rnds 20–23: Sc around.

Rnd 24: Through front loops only, (3 dc in next st, sl st in next st) 6 times. With tan, through back loops only of same rnd, sc around—12 sts.

Rnd 25: Sc around.

Rnd 26: Hdc 2 in each of next 4 sts, dc in each of rem 8 sts—16 sts.

Rnd 27: Sc in next st, 2 hdc in each of next 6 sts, sc in each of rem 9 sts—22 sts.

Rnd 28: Sc in each of next 3 sts, 2 hdc in each of next 8 sts, sc in each of rem 11 sts—30 sts.

Rnd 29: (Sc in each of next 4 sts, 2 sc in following st) 6 times—36 sts.

Rnd 30: (Sc in each of next 5 sts, 2 sc in following st) 6 times—42 sts.

Rnd 31: (Sc in each of next 6 sts, 2 sc in following st) 6 times—48 sts.

Rnds 32–34: Sc around.

Rnd 35: (Sc in each of next 6 sts, sc2tog) 6 times—42 sts.

Rnd 36: (Sc in each of next 5 sts, sc2tog) 6 times—36 sts.

Rnd 37: (Sc in each of next 4 sts, sc2tog) 6 times—30 sts.

Rnd 38: (Sc in each of next 3 sts, sc2tog) 6 times—24 sts.

Rnd 39: (Sc in each of next 2 sts, sc2tog) 6 times—18 sts.

Rnd 40: (Sc in next st, sc2tog) 6 times—12 sts.

Rnd 41: Sc in every other st—6 sts.

Fasten off, leaving a long tail for sewing.

»Legs

Make 2.

With yellow gold, make a magic circle.

Rnd 1: Work 4 sc in ring.

Rnd 2: *Sc 2 in next sc; rep from * around—8 sts.

Rnd 3: (Sc in next st, 2 sc in following st) 4 times—12 sts.

Rnd 4: Sc in next st, (3 hdc in next st, sl st in next st) 2 times; 3 dc in next st, sc in each of rem 6 sts—18 sts.

Rnd 5: Through back loops only and skipping sl sts, (sc in each of next 2 sts, sc2tog) 4 times—12 sts.

Rnd 6: (Sc in each of next 2 sts, sc2tog) 3 times—9 sts.

Rnd 7: Sc in each of next 3 sts, sc2tog 2 times, sc in each of rem 2 sts—7 sts.

Rnds 8–14: Sc around.

Fasten off, leaving a long tail for sewing.

»Tail Feathers

Go as crazy with colors as you want, as long as you make 7 tail feathers! I made 1 in moss green and 2 each in red, orange, and yellow gold.

With appropriate color, ch 17.

Hdc in 3rd ch from hook and in each of next 13 ch, 2 hdc in last ch. Turn foundation ch. On opposite side of foundation ch, 2 hdc in first ch, hdc in each of next 14 ch, sl st to first hdc.

Fasten off, leaving a long tail for sewing.

»Assembly

Sew snood to beak, making sure end dangles at bottom. With yellow gold, embroider buckle on hat. Lightly stuff hat and sew to head. Sew beak and snood to head between eyes. Stuff head, neck, and body. Arrange tail feathers in a fan and sew together. Sew tail to body. Stuff legs firmly. Sew legs to body. Weave in ends.

Sew the snood around one side of the beak.

Sew the tail feathers, overlapping them at the bottom to make a fan shape.

» Snowie Owl »

Snowie the owl stands tall and proud. His simple pattern and shape are given personality with a cute heart-shaped appliqué. Although his colors are just blue and cream, he remains one of the most gorgeous and regal snow owls there is.

Snowie Owl

> **Skill Level:** Easy
> **Finished Size:** 9½" tall

» Materials

See page 60 for more about yarns.

Yarn:

Light worsted- or DK-weight 4-ply acrylic yarn (3)

160 yds in cream for head and body

70 yds in blue for wings, ears, beak, and heart birthmark

10 yds in white for eyes

5 yds in brown for pupils

Hooks and Notions:

US Size F-5 (3.75 mm) crochet hook

Stitch marker, fiberfill stuffing, tapestry needle

» Ears

Make 2.

With blue, make a magic circle (page 61).

Rnd 1: Work 7 sc in ring.

Rnd 2: *Sc 2 in next sc; rep from * around—14 sts.

Rnd 3: Hdc in each of next 4 sts, 2 hdc in same st 7 times, hdc in each of rem 3 sts—21 sts.

Fasten off, leaving a long tail for sewing.

» Eyes

Make 2.

With brown, make a magic circle.

Rnd 1: Work 4 sc in ring.

Rnd 2: *Sc 2 in next sc; rep from * around—8 sts.

Rnd 3: With white, (sc in next st, 2 sc in following st) 4 times—12 sts.

Rnd 4: (Sc in each of next 2 sts, 2 sc in following st) 4 times—16 sts.

Rnd 5: (Sc in each of next 3 sts, 2 sc in following st) 4 times—20 sts.

Fasten off, leaving a long tail for sewing.

» Beak

With blue, make a magic circle.

Rnd 1: Work 6 sc in ring.

Rnd 2: *Sc 2 in next sc; rep from * around—12 sts.

Rnd 3: Sc around.

Fasten off, leaving a long tail for sewing.

» Wings

Make 2.

With blue, make a magic circle.

Rnd 1: Work 7 sc in ring.

Rnd 2: *Sc 2 in next sc; rep from * around—14 sts.

Rnd 3: Sc 2 in each of next 2 sts, sc in each of next 4 sts, 2 sc in each of next 3 sts, sc in each of next 3 sts, 2 sc in each of next 2 sts—21 sts.

Rnd 4: (Hdc in next st, 2 hdc in next st) 2 times, hdc in each of next 4 sts, (hdc in next st, 2 hdc in next st) 3 times, hdc in each of next 3 sts, (hdc in next st, 2 hdc in next st) 2 times—28 sts.

Rnd 5: (Hdc in each of next 2 sts, 2 hdc in next st) 2 times, hdc in each of next 4 sts, (hdc in each of next 2 sts, 2 hdc in next st) 3 times, hdc in each of next 3 sts, (hdc in each of next 2 sts, 2 hdc in next st) 2 times—35 sts.

Top view of ear.

Wing stitched to Snowie's side.

Rnd 6: (Hdc in each of next 3 sts, 2 hdc in next st) 2 times, hdc in each of next 4 sts, (hdc in each of next 3 sts, 2 hdc in next st) 3 times, hdc in each of next 3 sts, (hdc in each of next 3 sts, 2 hdc in next st) 2 times—42 sts.

Rnd 7: (Hdc in each of next 4 sts, 2 hdc in next st) 2 times, hdc in each of next 4 sts, (hdc in each of next 4 sts, 2 hdc in next st) 3 times, hdc in each of next 3 sts, (hdc in each of next 4 sts, 2 hdc in next st) 2 times—49 sts.

Huggable Amigurumi

Stitch the heart in place on Snowie's chest.

Rnd 8: (Hdc in each of next 5 sts, 2 hdc in next st) 2 times, hdc in each of next 3 sts, sc in each of next 7 sts, 2 dc in next st, (dc, ch, dc) in next st, 2 dc in next st, sc in each of next 8 sts, hdc in each of next 4 sts, (hdc in each of next 5 sts, 2 hdc in next st) 2 times—57 sts.

Fasten off, leaving a long tail for sewing.

» Head and Body

With cream, make a magic circle.

Rnd 1: Work 6 sc in ring.

Rnd 2: *Sc 2 in next sc; rep from * around—12 sts.

Rnd 3: (Sc in next st, 2 sc in following st) 6 times—18 sts.

Rnd 4: (Sc in each of next 2 sts, 2 sc in following st) 6 times—24 sts.

Rnd 5: (Sc in each of next 3 sts, 2 sc in following st) 6 times—30 sts.

Rnd 6: (Sc in each of next 4 sts, 2 sc in following st) 6 times—36 sts.

Rnd 7: (Sc in each of next 5 sts, 2 sc in following st) 6 times—42 sts.

Rnd 8: (Sc in each of next 6 sts, 2 sc in following st) 6 times—48 sts.

Rnds 9–20: Sc around.

Rnd 21: (Sc in each of next 6 sts, sc2tog) 6 times—42 sts.

Rnd 22: (Sc in each of next 5 sts, sc2tog) 6 times—36 sts.

Rnd 23: Through front loops only, (sc in each of next 5 sts, 2 sc in following st) 6 times—42 sts.

Rnd 24: (Sc in each of next 6 sts, 2 sc in following st) 6 times—48 sts.

Rnd 25: (Sc in each of next 7 sts, 2 sc in following st) 6 times—54 sts.

Rnd 26: (Sc in each of next 8 sts, 2 sc in following st) 6 times—60 sts.

Rnds 27–49: Sc around.

Rnd 50: Dc 2 in same st twice, sc in each of next 56 sts, 2 dc in each of rem 2 sts—64 sts.

Rnd 51: Sc2tog 2 times, sc in each of next 56 sts, sc2tog 2 times—60 sts.

Rnd 52: (Sc in each of next 8 sts, sc2tog) 6 times—54 sts.

Rnd 53: (Sc in each of next 7 sts, sc2tog) 6 times—48 sts.

Rnd 54: (Sc in each of next 6 sts, sc2tog) 6 times—42 sts.

Rnd 55: (Sc in each of next 5 sts, sc2tog) 6 times—36 sts.

Rnd 56: (Sc in each of next 4 sts, sc2tog) 6 times—30 sts.

Rnd 57: (Sc in each of next 3 sts, sc2tog) 6 times—24 sts.

Rnd 58: (Sc in each of next 2 sts, sc2tog) 6 times—18 sts.

Rnd 59: (Sc in next st, sc2tog) 6 times—12 sts.

Rnd 60: (Sc in next st, sc2tog) 4 times—8 sts.

Fasten off, leaving a long tail for sewing.

» Heart Appliqué

With blue, make a magic circle.

Rnd 1: Work 6 sc in ring.

Rnd 2: *Sc 2 in next sc; rep from * around—12 sts.

Rnd 3: (Sc in next st, 2 sc in following st) 6 times—18 sts.

Rnd 4: (Sc in each of next 2 sts, 2 sc in following st) 6 times—24 sts.

Rnd 5: Sc in each of first 5 sts, hdc in next st, dc in next st, 2 dc in next st, ch 2, 2 dc in next st, dc in next st, hdc in next st, sl st, hdc in next st, dc in next st, 2 dc in next st, ch 2, 2 dc in next st, dc in next st, hdc in next st, sc in each of rem 6 sts—32 sts.

Fasten off, leaving a long tail for sewing.

» Assembly

Sew ears to head. Sew eyes in place, leaving space for beak. Lightly stuff beak and attach it to head between eyes. Sew heart and wings to body. Stuff. Weave in ends.

» George Lion »

"Roar," says George! Be not afraid, since his roar is not meant to scare, but to welcome you to his magical kingdom. His moss-green mane and perfectly tan body make him the most handsome lion out there. His pattern is fairly easy, with only the mane to challenge your skills.

Huggable Amigurumi

Skill Level: Easy
Finished Size: 10½" tall

Materials

See page 60 for more about yarns.

Yarn:

Light worsted- or DK-weight 4-ply acrylic yarn (3)

170 yds in tan for head, ears, body, arms, legs, and tail

50 yds in chocolate brown for trim

30 yds in moss green for mane and tail

Hooks and Notions:

US Size F-5 (3.75 mm) crochet hook

2 buttons, 20 mm diameter, for eyes

Stitch marker, fiberfill stuffing, tapestry needle

Ears

Make 2.

With tan, make a magic circle (page 61).

Rnd 1: Work 6 sc in ring.

Rnd 2: *Sc 2 in next sc; rep from * around—12 sts.

Rnd 3: (Sc in next st, 2 sc in following st) 6 times—18 sts.

Rnds 4 and 5: Sc around.

Rnd 6: (Sc in next st, sc2tog) 6 times—12 sts.

Fasten off, leaving a long tail for sewing.

Mane

With moss green, ch 62, join in a ring.

Rnd 1: Through back loops only, dc in each ch around—62 sts.

Rnd 2: Through front loops only of foundation ch, (4 dc in next st, sl st in following st) 31 times—155 sts.

Rnd 3: Working in 62 dc of rnd 1, [2 sc in next st, hdc in next st, 2 dc in next st, ch 3, sl st in base of ch-3 (picot made), 2 dc in next st, hdc in next st, 2 sc in next st] 10 times, sl st in last 2 sts—102 sts.

Fasten off, leaving a long tail for sewing.

Head

With tan, make a magic circle.

Rnd 1: Work 6 sc in ring.

Rnd 2: *Sc 2 in next sc; rep from * around—12 sts.

Rnd 3: (Sc in next st, 2 sc in following st) 6 times—18 sts.

Rnd 4: (Sc in each of next 2 sts, 2 sc in following st) 6 times—24 sts.

Rnd 5: (Sc in each of next 3 sts, 2 sc in following st) 6 times—30 sts.

Rnd 6: (Sc in each of next 4 sts, 2 sc in following st) 6 times—36 sts.

Rnd 7: (Sc in each of next 5 sts, 2 sc in following st) 6 times—42 sts.

Rnd 8: (Sc in each of next 6 sts, 2 sc in following st) 6 times—48 sts.

Rnd 9: (Sc in each of next 7 sts, 2 sc in following st) 6 times—54 sts.

Rnds 10–20: Sc around.

Rnd 21: (Sc in each of next 8 sts, 2 sc in following st) 6 times—60 sts.

Rnd 22: Sc around.

Rnd 23: (Sc in each of next 8 sts, sc2tog) 6 times—54 sts.

Rnd 24: (Sc in each of next 7 sts, sc2tog) 6 times—48 sts.

Rnd 25: (Sc in each of next 6 sts, sc2tog) 6 times—42 sts.

Rnd 26: (Sc in each of next 5 sts, sc2tog) 6 times—36 sts.

Rnd 27: (Sc in each of next 4 sts, sc2tog) 6 times—30 sts.

Rnd 28: (Sc in each of next 3 sts, sc2tog) 6 times—24 sts.

Rnd 29: (Sc in each of next 2 sts, sc2tog) 6 times—18 sts.

Fasten off.

» Body

With tan, make a magic circle.

Rnd 1: Work 6 sc in ring.

Rnd 2: *Sc 2 in next sc; rep from * around—12 sts.

Rnd 3: (Sc in next st, 2 sc in following st) 6 times—18 sts.

Rnd 4: (Sc in each of next 2 sts, 2 sc in following st) 6 times—24 sts.

Rnd 5: (Sc in each of next 3 sts, 2 sc in following st) 6 times—30 sts.

Rnd 6: (Sc in each of next 4 sts, 2 sc in following st) 6 times—36 sts.

Rnd 7: (Sc in each of next 5 sts, 2 sc in following st) 6 times—42 sts.

Rnd 8: (Sc in each of next 6 sts, 2 sc in following st) 6 times—48 sts.

Rnd 9: (Sc in each of next 7 sts, 2 sc in following st) 6 times—54 sts.

Rnds 10–13: Sc around.

Rnd 14: (Sc in each of next 7 sts, sc2tog) 6 times—48 sts.

Rnds 15–17: Sc around.

Rnd 18: (Sc in each of next 6 sts, sc2tog) 6 times—42 sts.

Rnds 19 and 20: Sc around.

Rnd 21: (Sc in each of next 5 sts, sc2tog) 6 times—36 sts.

Rnds 22–24: Sc around.

Rnd 25: (Sc in each of next 4 sts, sc2tog) 6 times—30 sts.

Rnds 26–28: Sc around.

Rnd 29: (Sc in each of next 3 sts, sc2tog) 6 times—24 sts.

Rnds 30 and 31: Sc around.

Rnd 32: (Sc in each of next 2 sts, sc2tog) 6 times—18 sts.

Fasten off, leaving a long tail for sewing.

» Arms

Make 2.

With chocolate brown, make a magic circle.

Rnd 1: Work 6 sc in ring.

Rnd 2: *Sc 2 in next sc; rep from * around—12 sts.

Rnd 3: (Sc in next st, 2 sc in following st) 6 times—18 sts.

Rnds 4–6: Sc around.

Rnds 7–14: With tan, sc around.

Rnd 15: (Sc in next st, sc2tog) 6 times—12 sts.

Rnds 16–26: Sc around.

Fasten off, leaving a long tail for sewing.

» Legs

Make 2.

With chocolate brown, make a magic circle.

Rnd 1: Work 6 sc in ring.

Rnd 2: *Sc 2 in next sc; rep from * around—12 sts.

Rnd 3: (Sc in next st, 2 sc in following st) 6 times—18 sts.

Rnd 4: (Sc in each of next 2 sts, 2 sc in following st) 6 times—24 sts.

Rnd 5: (Sc in each of next 3 sts, 2 sc in following st) 6 times—30 sts.

Rnd 6: (Sc in each of next 4 sts, 2 sc in following st) 6 times—36 sts.

Rnd 7: Through back loops only, sc in each of next 14 sts, sc2tog 4 times, sc in each of rem 14 sts—32 sts.

Rnd 8: Sc in each of next 12 sts, sc2tog 4 times, sc in each of rem 12 sts—28 sts.

Rnd 9: Sc in each of next 10 sts, sc2tog 4 times, sc in each of rem 10 sts—24 sts.

George's tail is a simple crochet chain made with 2 yarns held together.

Rnd 10: Sc in each of next 6 sts, sc2tog 6 times, sc in each of rem 6 sts—18 sts.

Rnd 11: Sc around.

Rnds 12–21: With tan, sc around—18 sts.

Rnd 22: Sc in each of next 6 sts, 2 sc in each of next 6 sts, sc in each of rem 6 sts—24 sts.

Rnd 23: Sc in each of next 6 sts, sc2tog 6 times, sc in each of rem 6 sts—18 sts.

Fasten off, leaving a long tail for sewing.

» Tail

With tan and moss green held tog, ch 40 loosely.

Fasten off, leaving a long tail for sewing.

» Assembly

Sew ears to mane, and then sew mane to head. Sew eyes in place. With chocolate brown, embroider a triangular nose as shown.

Stuff head firmly. Stuff arms and legs. Sew tail (unstuffed), arms, and legs in place on body. Stuff body firmly. Sew head to body. Weave in ends.

» Stella Squirrel »

Her jeweled eyes shine, but it's her uniquely shaped tail that truly makes Stella stand out. Made with simple shaping techniques, little Stella is a one-of-a-kind amigurumi squirrel.

Skill Level: Easy
Finished Size: 12" tall

>> Materials

See page 60 for more about yarns.

Yarn:
Light worsted- or DK-weight 4-ply acrylic yarn (3)
180 yds in brown for ears, head, body, arms, and legs
80 yds in olive green for tail
45 yds in white for tummy

Hooks and Notions:
US Size F-5 (3.75 mm) crochet hook
2 jeweled buttons, 20 mm diameter, for eyes
Stitch marker, fiberfill stuffing, tapestry needle

>> Ears

Make 2.

With brown, make a magic circle (page 61).

Rnd 1: Work 5 sc in ring.

Rnd 2: *Sc 2 in next sc; rep from * around—10 sts.

Rnd 3: (Sc in next st, 2 sc in following st) 5 times—15 sts.

Rnd 4: Sc around.

Rnd 5: (Sc in each of next 2 sts, 2 sc in following st) 5 times—20 sts.

Rnds 6–10: Sc around.

Fasten off, leaving a long tail for sewing.

>> Head

With brown, make a magic circle.

Rnd 1: Work 6 sc in ring.

Rnd 2: *Sc 2 in next sc; rep from * around—12 sts.

Rnd 3: (Sc in next st, 2 sc in following st) 6 times—18 sts.

Rnd 4: (Sc in each of next 2 sts, 2 sc in following st) 6 times—24 sts.

Rnds 5 and 6: Sc around.

Rnd 7: (Sc in each of next 3 sts, 2 sc in following st) 6 times—30 sts.

Rnd 8: (Sc in each of next 4 sts, 2 sc in following st) 6 times—36 sts.

Rnd 9: Sc around.

Rnd 10: (Sc in each of next 5 sts, 2 sc in following st) 6 times—42 sts.

Rnd 11: (Sc in each of next 6 sts, 2 sc in following st) 6 times—48 sts.

Rnd 12: Sc around.

Rnd 13: (Sc in each of next 7 sts, 2 sc in following st) 6 times—54 sts.

Rnd 14: (Sc in each of next 8 sts, 2 sc in following st) 6 times—60 sts.

Rnds 15–22: Sc around.

Rnd 23: (Sc in each of next 8 sts, sc2tog) 6 times—54 sts.

Rnd 24: (Sc in each of next 7 sts, sc2tog) 6 times—48 sts.

Rnd 25: (Sc in each of next 6 sts, sc2tog) 6 times—42 sts.

Rnd 26: (Sc in each of next 5 sts, sc2tog) 6 times—36 sts.

Rnd 27: (Sc in each of next 4 sts, sc2tog) 6 times—30 sts.

Rnd 28: (Sc in each of next 3 sts, sc2tog) 6 times—24 sts.

Stuff firmly.

Rnd 29: (Sc in each of next 2 sts, sc2tog) 6 times—18 sts.

Rnd 30: (Sc in next st, sc2tog) 6 times—12 sts.

Rnd 31: Sc in every other st—6 sts.

White tummy is crocheted separately and sewn on during assembly.

Fasten off, leaving a long tail for sewing.

>> Tummy

With white, ch 13.

Row 1: Dc in 4th ch from hook and in each ch across, turn—11 sts.

Rows 2–13: Ch 3 (counts as dc), dc across.

Fasten off, leaving a long tail for sewing.

>> Arms

Make 2.

With brown, make a magic circle.

Rnd 1: Work 5 sc in ring.

Rnd 2: *Sc 2 in next sc; rep from * around—10 sts.

Rnd 3: (Sc in next st, 2 sc in following st) 5 times—15 sts.

Rnd 4: (Sc in each of next 2 sts, 2 sc in following st) 5 times—20 sts.

Rnds 5–13: Sc around.

Rnd 14: (Sc in each of next 2 sts, sc2tog) 5 times—15 sts.

Rnds 15–19: Sc around.

Rnd 20: (Sc in next st, sc2tog) 5 times—10 sts.

Rnds 21–23: Sc around.

Fasten off, leaving a long tail for sewing.

Huggable Amigurumi

» Body

With brown, make a magic circle.

Rnd 1: Work 6 sc in ring.

Rnd 2: *Sc 2 in next sc; rep from * around—12 sts.

Rnd 3: (Sc in next st, 2 sc in following st) 6 times—18 sts.

Rnd 4: (Sc in each of next 2 sts, 2 sc in following st) 6 times—24 sts.

Rnd 5: (Sc in each of next 3 sts, 2 sc in following st) 6 times—30 sts.

Rnd 6: (Sc in each of next 4 sts, 2 sc in following st) 6 times—36 sts.

Rnd 7: (Sc in each of next 5 sts, 2 sc in following st) 6 times—42 sts.

Rnd 8: (Sc in each of next 6 sts, 2 sc in following st) 6 times—48 sts.

Rnd 9: (Sc in each of next 7 sts, 2 sc in following st) 6 times—54 sts.

Rnds 10–12: Sc around.

Rnd 13: (Sc in each of next 7 sts, sc2tog) 6 times—48 sts.

Rnds 14–16: Sc around.

Rnd 17: (Sc in each of next 6 sts, sc2tog) 6 times—42 sts.

Rnds 18–20: Sc around.

Rnd 21: (Sc in each of next 5 sts, sc2tog) 6 times—36 sts.

Rnds 22–24: Sc around.

Rnd 25: (Sc in each of next 4 sts, sc2tog) 6 times—30 sts.

Rnds 26 and 27: Sc around.

Rnd 28: (Sc in each of next 3 sts, sc2tog) 6 times—24 sts.

Rnds 29–31: Sc around.

Rnd 32: (Sc in each of next 2 sts, sc2tog) 6 times—18 sts.

Fasten off, leaving a long tail for sewing.

» Legs

Make 2.

With brown, make a magic circle.

Rnd 1: Work 6 sc in ring.

Rnd 2: *Sc 2 in next sc; rep from * around—12 sts.

Rnd 3: (Sc in next st, 2 sc in following st) 6 times—18 sts.

Rnd 4: (Sc in each of next 2 sts, 2 sc in following st) 6 times—24 sts.

Rnds 5–12: Sc around.

Rnd 13: (Sc in each of next 2 sts, sc2tog) 6 times—18 sts.

Rnds 14–18: Sc around.

Fasten off, leaving a long tail for sewing.

» Tail

With olive green, make a magic circle.

Rnd 1: Work 6 sc in ring.

Rnd 2: *Sc 2 in next sc; rep from * around—12 sts.

Rnd 3: (Sc in next st, 2 sc in following st) 6 times—18 sts.

Rnd 4: (Sc in each of next 2 sts, 2 sc in following st) 6 times—24 sts.

Rnd 5: (Sc in each of next 3 sts, 2 sc in following st) 6 times—30 sts.

Rnd 6: (Sc in each of next 4 sts, 2 sc in following st) 6 times—36 sts.

Rnd 7: (Sc in each of next 5 sts, 2 sc in following st) 6 times—42 sts.

Rnds 8–12: Sc around.

Rnd 13: Sc in each of next 15 sts, sc2tog 6 times, sc in each of rem 15 sts—36 sts.

Rnd 14: Sc in each of next 12 sts, sc2tog 6 times, sc in each of rem 12 sts—30 sts.

Rnd 15: Sc around.

Rnd 16: Sc in each of next 12 sts, 2 sc in next 6 sts, sc in each of rem 12 sts—36 sts.

Rnds 17–21: Sc around.

Rnd 22: Sc in each of next 12 sts, sc2tog 6 times, sc in each of rem 12 sts—30 sts.

Rnd 23: Sc in each of next 9 sts, sc2tog 6 times, sc in each of rem 9 sts—24 sts.

Rnd 24: Sc around.

Rnd 25: Sc in each of next 9 sts, 2 sc in next 6 sts, sc in each of rem 9 sts—30 sts.

Rnds 26–31: Sc around.

Rnd 32: (Sc in each of next 3 sts, sc2tog) 6 times—24 sts.

Rnd 33: (Sc in each of next 2 sts, sc2tog) 6 times—18 sts.

Rnd 34: (Sc in each of next 4 sts, sc2tog) 3 times—15 sts.

Rnd 35: (Sc in each of next 3 sts, sc2tog) 3 times—12 sts.

Rnd 36: (Sc in each of next 2 sts, sc2tog) 3 times—9 sts.

Fasten off, leaving a long tail for sewing.

» Assembly

With white, embroider a triangular nose with a line extending downward as shown on head. Sew eyes in place. Sew ears to head, folding slightly at base to shape.

Sew tummy to body. Stuff arms, legs, and tail, and sew in place on body. Stuff body. Sew head to body. Weave in ends.

» Sammie Seal »

Sammie's quirky colors will make you smile on a gloomy day. Her fun blue skin and pink flippers make her a darling that will brighten your mood.

Huggable Amigurumi

Skill Level: Easy
Finished Size: 9½" tall

>> Materials

See page 60 for more about yarns.

Yarn:

Light worsted- or DK-weight 4-ply acrylic yarn (3)

90 yds in powder blue for head and body

40 yds in pastel pink for flippers

30 yds in tan for muzzle

5 yds in black for embroidery

Hooks and Notions:

US Size F-5 (3.75 mm) crochet hook

2 buttons, 20 mm diameter, for eyes

Stitch marker, fiberfill stuffing, tapestry needle

>> Head

With powder blue, make a magic circle (page 61).

Rnd 1: Work 6 sc in ring.

Rnd 2: *Sc 2 sc in next sc; rep from * around—12 sts.

Rnd 3: (Sc in next st, 2 sc in following st) 6 times—18 sts.

Rnd 4: (Sc in each of next 2 sts, 2 sc in following st) 6 times—24 sts.

Rnd 5: (Sc in each of next 3 sts, 2 sc in following st) 6 times—30 sts.

Rnd 6: (Sc in each of next 4 sts, 2 sc in following st) 6 times—36 sts.

Rnd 7: (Sc in each of next 5 sts, 2 sc in following st) 6 times—42 sts.

Rnd 8: Sc around.

Rnd 9: (Sc in each of next 6 sts, 2 sc in following st) 6 times—48 sts.

Rnd 10: (Sc in each of next 7 sts, 2 sc in following st) 6 times—54 sts.

Rnd 11: (Sc in each of next 8 sts, 2 sc in following st) 6 times—60 sts.

Rnd 12: (Sc in each of next 9 sts, 2 sc in following st) 6 times—66 sts.

Rnds 13–24: Sc around.

Rnd 25: (Sc in each of next 10 sts, 2 sc in following st) 6 times—72 sts.

Rnd 26: (Sc in each of next 11 sts, 2 sc in following st) 6 times—78 sts.

Rnds 27 and 28: Sc around.

Rnd 29: (Sc in each of next 11 sts, sc2tog) 6 times—72 sts.

Rnd 30: (Sc in each of next 4 sts, sc2tog) 12 times—60 sts.

Rnd 31: (Sc in each of next 3 sts, sc2tog) 12 times—48 sts.

Rnd 32: (Sc in each of next 2 sts, sc2tog) 12 times—36 sts.

Rnd 33: (Sc in each of next 4 sts, sc2tog) 6 times—30 sts.

Rnd 34: (Sc in each of next 3 sts, sc2tog) 6 times—24 sts.

Rnd 35: (Sc in each of next 2 sts, sc2tog) 6 times—18 sts.

Rnd 36: (Sc in next st, sc2tog) 6 times—12 sts.

Fasten off, leaving a long tail for sewing.

The embroidery stitches on Sammie's muzzle.

Tail flippers.

Front flippers.

>> 48 >>

» Muzzle

With tan, ch 12.

Rnd 1: Sc in 2nd ch from hook and each of next 9 ch, 2 sc in last ch. Turn foundation ch. On opposite side of foundation ch, sc in each of next 10 ch, 2 sc in last ch—24 sts.

Rnd 2: Sc 2 in each of next 2 sts, sc in each of next 8 sts, 2 sc in each of next 4 sts, sc in each of next 8 sts, 2 sc in each of next 2 sts—32 sts.

Rnd 3: (Sc in next st, 2 sc in following st) 2 times, sc in each of next 8 sts, (sc in next st, 2 sc in following st) 4 times, sc in each of next 8 sts, (sc in next st, 2 sc in following st) 2 times—40 sts.

Rnd 4: (Sc in each of next 2 sts, 2 sc in following st) 2 times, sc in each of next 8 sts, (sc in each of next 2 sts, 2 sc in following st) 4 times, sc in each of next 8 sts, (sc in each of next 2 sts, 2 sc in following st) 2 times—48 sts.

Rnds 5–10: Sc around.

Rnd 11: (Sc in each of next 4 sts, sc2tog) 8 times—40 sts.

Fasten off, leaving a long tail for sewing.

» Body

With powder blue, make a magic circle.

Rnd 1: Work 6 sc in ring.

Rnd 2: *Sc 2 in next sc; rep from * around—12 sts.

Rnd 3: (Sc in next st, 2 sc in following st) 6 times—18 sts.

Rnd 4: (Sc in each of next 2 sts, 2 sc in following st) 6 times—24 sts.

Rnd 5: (Sc in each of next 3 sts, 2 sc in following st) 6 times—30 sts.

Rnd 6: (Sc in each of next 4 sts, 2 sc in following st) 6 times—36 sts.

Rnd 7: (Sc in each of next 5 sts, 2 sc in following st) 6 times—42 sts.

Rnds 8–12: Sc around.

Rnd 13: (Sc in each of next 5 sts, sc2tog) 6 times—36 sts.

Rnds 14–16: Sc around.

Rnd 17: (Sc in each of next 4 sts, sc2tog) 6 times—30 sts.

Rnds 18–22: Sc around.

Rnd 23: (Sc in each of next 3 sts, sc2tog) 6 times—24 sts.

Rnds 24–26: Sc around.

Fasten off, leaving a long tail for sewing.

» Front Flippers

Make 2.

With pastel pink, make a magic circle.

Rnd 1: Work 5 sc in ring.

Rnd 2: *Sc 2 in next sc; rep from * around—10 sts.

Rnd 3: (Sc in next st, 2 sc in following st) 5 times—15 sts.

Rnds 4 and 5: Sc around.

Rnd 6: Sc2tog 3 times, sc in each of next 9 sts—12 sts.

Rnd 7: Sc2tog 2 times, sc in each of next 8 sts—10 sts.

Rnds 8–15: Sc around.

Fasten off, leaving a long tail for sewing.

» Tail Flippers

Make 2.

With pastel pink, make a magic circle.

Rnd 1: Work 5 sc in ring.

Rnd 2: *Sc 2 in next sc; rep from * around—10 sts.

Rnd 3: Sc around.

Rnd 4: (Sc in next st, 2 sc in following st) 5 times—15 sts.

Rnd 5: (Sc in each of next 2 sts, 2 sc in following st) 5 times—20 sts.

Rnds 6–9: Sc around.

Rnd 10: (Sc in each of next 2 sts, sc2tog) 5 times—15 sts.

Rnd 11: Sc around.

Rnd 12: (Sc in next st, sc2tog) 5 times—10 sts.

Fasten off, leaving a long tail for sewing.

» Assembly

Embroider muzzle with black using a running stitch, making straight lines and small cross-stitches as shown.

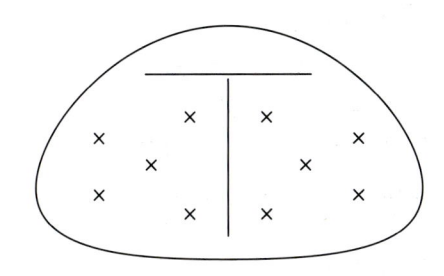

Stuff muzzle firmly and sew to head. Sew eyes in place. Sew tail flippers to bottom of body.

Sew front flippers to front of body at lower edge. Stuff head and body firmly. Sew head to body. Weave in ends.

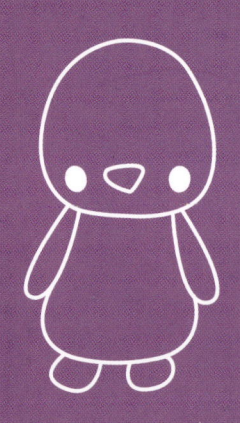

» Ellie Penguin »

Ellie has always been one of my favorite girl names, and what better way to honor the name than by combining my loves: pink, penguins, and crochet! Although she's different from her other penguin friends, she fully embraces her naturally pink body. Her pattern requires little sewing and is as simple as can be.

Skill Level: Easy
Finished Size: 9½" tall

» Materials

See page 60 for more about yarns.

Yarn:

Light worsted- or DK-weight 4-ply acrylic yarn (3)

90 yds in pink for body

50 yds in gray for head and wings

30 yds in yellow gold for feet and beak

Hooks and Notions:

US Size F-5 (3.75 mm) crochet hook

2 safety eyes, 16.5 mm diameter

Stitch marker, fiberfill stuffing, tapestry needle

» Beak

With yellow gold, ch 5.

Rnd 1: Sc in 2nd ch from hook and in each of next 2 ch, 2 sc in last ch. Turn foundation ch. On opposite side of ch, sc in each of first 3 ch, 2 sc in last ch—10 sts.

Rnd 2: (Sc in next st, 2 sc in following st) 5 times—15 sts.

Rnd 3: Sc around.

Rnd 4: (Sc in each of next 2 sts, 2 sc in following st) 5 times—20 sts.

Fasten off, leaving a long tail for sewing.

» Wings

Make 2.

With gray, make a magic circle (page 61).

Rnd 1: Work 6 sc in ring.

Rnd 2: *Sc 2 in next sc; rep from * around—12 sts.

Rnd 3: Sc 2 in each of next 2 sts, sc in each of next 3 sts, 2 sc in each of next 3 sts, sc in each of next 3 sts, 2 sc in last st—18 sts.

Rnd 4: (Sc in next st, 2 sc in following st) 2 times, sc in each of next 3 sts, (sc in next st, 2 sc in following st) 3 times, sc in each of next 4 sts, 2 sc in last st—24 sts.

Rnd 5: (Sc in each of next 2 sts, 2 sc in following st) 2 times, sc in each of next 3 sts, (sc in each of next 2 sts, 2 sc in following st) 3 times, sc in each of next 5 sts, 2 sc in last st—30 sts.

Rnd 6: Sc in each of first 9 sts, (hdc in next st, 2 hdc in next st) 6 times, sc in each of next 9 sts—36 sts.

Rnd 7: Sc in each of first 12 sts, (hdc in next st, 2 hdc in next st) 6 times, sc in each of next 12 sts—42 sts.

Fasten off, leaving a long tail for sewing.

» Head and Body

With gray, make a magic circle.

Rnd 1: Work 7 sc in ring.

Rnd 2: *Sc 2 in next sc; rep from * around—14 sts.

Rnd 3: (Sc in next st, 2 sc in following st) 7 times—21 sts.

Rnd 4: (Sc in each of next 2 sts, 2 sc in following st) 7 times—28 sts.

Rnd 5: (Sc in each of next 3 sts, 2 sc in following st) 7 times—35 sts.

Rnd 6: (Sc in each of next 4 sts, 2 sc in following st) 7 times—42 sts.

Rnd 7: (Sc in each of next 5 sts, 2 sc in following st) 7 times—49 sts.

Sew the wings around the top curve, leaving the bottom free.

Sew the beak to the head between the eyes.

Rnd 8: (Sc in each of next 6 sts, 2 sc in following st) 7 times—56 sts.

Rnds 9–24: Sc around.

Rnd 25: (Sc in each of next 7 sts, 2 sc in following st) 7 times—63 sts.

Rnd 26: Sc around.

Rnd 27: (Sc in each of next 7 sts, sc2tog) 7 times—56 sts.

Rnd 28: (Sc in each of next 6 sts, sc2tog) 7 times—49 sts.

Rnd 29: (Sc in each of next 5 sts, sc2tog) 7 times—42 sts.

Top view of foot.

Bottom view.

Rnd 30: (Sc in each of next 4 sts, sc2tog) 7 times—35 sts.

Rnd 31: (Sc in each of next 3 sts, sc2tog) 7 times—28 sts.

Rnd 32: (Sc in each of next 2 sts, sc2tog) 7 times—21 sts.

Stuff beak firmly. Sew to head. Attach safety eyes approx ¾" from beak. Start stuffing head.

Rnd 33: With pink, (sc in next st, sc2tog) 7 times—14 sts.

Rnd 34: Sc around.

Rnd 35: (Sc in next st, 2 sc in following st) 7 times—21 sts.

Rnd 36: (Sc in each of next 2 sts, 2 sc in following st) 7 times—28 sts.

Rnd 37: (Sc in each of next 3 sts, 2 sc in following st) 7 times—35 sts.

Rnd 38: (Sc in each of next 4 sts, 2 sc in following st) 7 times—42 sts.

Rnds 39–42: Sc around.

Rnd 43: (Sc in each of next 5 sts, 2 sc in following st) 7 times—49 sts.

Sew wings to body, with ends aligned with rnd 35.

Rnds 44–46: Sc around.

Rnd 47: (Sc in each of next 6 sts, 2 sc in following st) 7 times—56 sts.

Rnds 48–51: Sc around.

Rnd 52: (Sc in each of next 7 sts, 2 sc in following st) 7 times—63 sts.

Rnds 53–56: Sc around.

Rnd 57: (Sc in each of next 7 sts, sc2tog) 7 times—56 sts.

Rnd 58: (Sc in each of next 6 sts, sc2tog) 7 times—49 sts.

Rnd 59: (Sc in each of next 5 sts, sc2tog) 7 times—42 sts.

Rnd 60: (Sc in each of next 4 sts, sc2tog) 7 times—35 sts.

Rnd 61: (Sc in each of next 3 sts, sc2tog) 7 times—28 sts.

Rnd 62: (Sc in each of next 2 sts, sc2tog) 7 times—21 sts.

Rnd 63: (Sc in next st, sc2tog) 7 times—14 sts.

Rnd 64: Sc in every other st—7 sts.

Fasten off, leaving a long tail for sewing.

» Feet

Make 2.

With yellow gold, make a magic circle.

Rnd 1: Work 6 sc in ring.

Rnd 2: *Sc 2 in next sc; rep from * around—12 sts.

Rnd 3: (Sc in next st, 2 sc in following st) 6 times—18 sts.

Rnd 4: (Sc in each of next 2 sts, 2 sc in following st) 6 times—24 sts.

Rnd 5: Sc in each of next 6 sts, hdc in next st, 2 hdc in next st, dc in next st, 2 dc in next st, sl st in next st, 2 dc in next st, dc in next st, 2 hdc in next st, hdc in next st, sc in each of rem 9 sts—28 sts.

Fasten off, leaving a long tail for sewing.

» Assembly

Stuff rest of body firmly. Sew feet to bottom of body. Weave in ends.

» Rocco Raccoon »

Little Rocco's color scheme makes him a stylish raccoon. Using simple shaping techniques and decorative long single crochet stitches, Rocco's pattern is easy to follow and quick to work up.

Huggable Amigurumi

Skill Level: Easy
Finished Size: 9" tall

Materials

See page 60 for more about yarns.

Yarn:
Light worsted- or DK-weight 4-ply acrylic yarn (3)
80 yds in gray for head, ears, arms, legs, tail, and body
45 yds in white for tummy, eyes, and muzzle
35 yds in black for trim
5 yds in light gray for eyes

Hooks and Notions:
US Size F-5 (3.75 mm) crochet hook
2 safety eyes, 14 mm diameter
Stitch marker, fiberfill stuffing, tapestry needle

Ears

Make 2.

With black, make a magic circle (page 61).

Rnd 1: Work 4 sc in ring.
Rnd 2: *Sc 2 in next sc; rep from * around—8 sts.
Rnd 3: (Sc in next st, 2 sc in following st) 4 times—12 sts.
Rnd 4: With gray, (sc in next st, 2 sc in following st) 6 times—18 sts.
Rnd 5: Sc around.
Rnd 6: (Sc in each of next 2 sts, 2 sc in following st) 6 times—24 sts.
Rnd 7: Sc around.

Fasten off, leaving a long tail for sewing.

Head

With gray, make a magic circle.

Rnd 1: Work 6 sc in ring.
Rnd 2: *Sc 2 in next sc; rep from * around—12 sts.
Rnd 3: (Sc in next st, 2 sc in following st) 6 times—18 sts.
Rnd 4: (Sc in each of next 2 sts, 2 sc in following st) 6 times—24 sts.
Rnd 5: (Sc in each of next 3 sts, 2 sc in following st) 6 times—30 sts.
Rnd 6: (Sc in each of next 4 sts, 2 sc in following st) 6 times—36 sts.
Rnd 7: (Sc in each of next 5 sts, 2 sc in following st) 6 times—42 sts.
Rnd 8: (Sc in each of next 6 sts, 2 sc in following st) 6 times—48 sts.
Rnds 9–18: Sc around.
Rnd 19: With white, through front loops only, (sc in each of next 5 sts, 2 sc in following st) 8 times—56 sts.
Rnd 20: Sc around.
Rnd 21: (Sc in each of next 5 sts, sc2tog) 8 times—48 sts.
Rnd 22: (Sc in each of next 4 sts, sc2tog) 8 times—40 sts.
Rnd 23: (Sc in each of next 3 sts, sc2tog) 8 times—32 sts.
Rnd 24: (Sc in each of next 2 sts, sc2tog) 8 times—24 sts.
Rnd 25: (Sc in next st, sc2tog) 8 times—16 sts.

Fasten off.

Stuff the tail before attaching.

Muzzle

With black, make a magic circle.

Rnd 1: Work 4 sc in ring.
Rnd 2: Sc in each of next 2 sts, 2 sc in each of next 2 sts—6 sts.
Rnd 3: With white, sc around.
Rnd 4: *Sc 2 in next sc; rep from * around—12 sts.
Rnd 5: (Sc in next st, 2 sc in following st) 6 times—18 sts.

Fasten off, leaving a long tail for sewing.

Eyes

Make 2.

With light gray, make a magic circle.

Rnd 1: Work 5 sc in ring.
Rnd 2: *Sc 2 in next sc; rep from * around—10 sts.
Rnd 3: Sc in next st, 2 hdc in next st, (hdc in next st, 2 hdc in next st) 3 times, sc in next st, 2 sc in last st—15 sts.
Rnd 4: With black, (sc in each of next 2 sts, 2 sc in following st) 5 times—20 sts.
Rnd 5: With white, (3 dc in next st, sl st in next st) 2 times, sc in each of rem 16 sts—24 sts.

Fasten off, leaving a long tail for sewing.

Arms

Make 2.

With black, make a magic circle.

Rnd 1: Work 5 sc in ring.

Rnd 2: *Sc 2 in next sc; rep from * around—10 sts.

Rnds 3 and 4: Sc around.

Rnd 5: (Sc in each of next 3 sts, sc2tog) 2 times—8 sts.

Rnds 6–11: With gray, sc around.

Fasten off, leaving a long tail for sewing.

Tummy

With white, make a magic circle.

Rnd 1: Work 5 sc in ring.

Rnd 2: *Sc 2 in next sc; rep from * around—10 sts.

Rnd 3: (Sc in next st, 2 sc in following st) 5 times—15 sts.

Rnd 4: (Sc in each of next 2 sts, 2 sc in following st) 5 times—20 sts.

Rnd 5: (Sc in each of next 3 sts, 2 sc in following st) 5 times—25 sts.

Fasten off, leaving a long tail for sewing.

Body

With gray, make a magic circle.

Rnd 1: Work 6 sc in ring.

Rnd 2: *Sc 2 in next sc; rep from * around—12 sts.

Rnd 3: (Sc in next st, 2 sc in following st) 6 times—18 sts.

Rnd 4: (Sc in each of next 2 sts, 2 sc in following st) 6 times—24 sts.

Rnd 5: (Sc in each of next 3 sts, 2 sc in following st) 6 times—30 sts.

Rnd 6: (Sc in each of next 4 sts, 2 sc in following st) 6 times—36 sts.

Rnds 7–12: Sc around.

Rnd 13: (Sc in each of next 4 sts, sc2tog) 6 times—30 sts.

Rnds 14 and 15: Sc around.

Rnd 16: (Sc in each of next 3 sts, sc2tog) 6 times—24 sts.

Rnds 17 and 18: Sc around.

Fasten off, leaving a long tail for sewing.

Legs

Make 2.

With black, make a magic circle.

Rnd 1: Work 6 sc in ring.

Rnd 2: *Sc 2 in next sc; rep from * around—12 sts.

Rnd 3: (Sc in next st, 2 sc in following st) 6 times—18 sts.

Rnd 4: Through back loops only, sc in each of next 6 sts, sc2tog 3 times, sc in each of rem 6 sts—15 sts.

Rnd 5: Sc in each of next 4 sts, sc2tog 3 times, sc in each of rem 5 sts—12 sts.

Rnds 6–8: Sc around.

Rnd 9: With gray, (sc in next st, long sc in next st) 6 times—12 sts.

Rnd 10: Sc around.

Rnd 11: (Sc in each of next 2 sts, sc2tog) 3 times—9 sts.

Rnds 12 and 13: Sc around.

Fasten off, leaving a long tail for sewing.

Tail

With black, make a magic circle.

Rnd 1: Work 5 sc in ring.

Rnd 2: *Sc 2 in next sc; rep from * around—10 sts.

Rnd 3: (Sc in each of next 4 sts, 2 sc in following st) 2 times—12 sts.

Rnd 4: (Sc in each of next 2 sts, 2 sc in following st) 4 times—16 sts.

Rnd 5: With gray, (sc in next st, long sc in next st) 8 times—16 sts.

Rnd 6: (Sc in each of next 3 sts, 2 sc in following st) 4 times—20 sts.

Rnd 7: (Sc in each of next 4 sts, 2 sc in following st) 4 times—24 sts.

Rnd 8: With black, (sc in next st, long sc in next st) 12 times—24 sts.

Rnd 9: (Sc in each of next 3 sts, 2 sc in following st) 6 times—30 sts.

Rnd 10: Sc around.

Rnd 11: With gray, (sc in next st, long sc in next st) 15 times—30 sts.

Rnd 12: (Sc in each of next 3 sts, sc2tog) 6 times—24 sts.

Rnd 13: Sc around.

Rnd 14: (Sc in each of next 4 sts, sc2tog) 4 times—20 sts.

Rnd 15: With black, (sc in next st, long sc in next st) 10 times—20 sts.

Rnd 16: Sl st in each of next 4 sts, sc2tog 2 times, sc in each of next 4 sts, sc2tog 2 times, sl st in each of rem 4 sts—16 sts.

Fasten off, leaving a long tail for sewing.

Assembly

Sew ears to head. Lightly stuff muzzle. Sew to head. Attach safety eyes to center of eye patches and sew in place. Stuff head. Stuff body, tail, arms, and legs. Sew arms, legs, and tail to body.

Sew head and tummy to body. Weave in ends.

» Gunny Bear »

Gunny Bear is ready for his winter expedition across the Atlantic! His pattern may seem long, but its simplicity will make up for the length. His huggable size makes him the perfect cuddly companion.

> Skill Level: Easy
> Finished Size: 10½" tall

» Materials

See page 60 for more about yarns.

Yarn:

Light worsted- or DK-weight 4-ply acrylic yarn (3)

250 yds in off-white for arms and head

170 yds in white for hat, ears, muzzle, and trim

150 yds in navy for overalls and trim

2 yds in pink for trim

Hooks and Notions:

US Size F-5 (3.75 mm) crochet hook

2 buttons, 36 mm diameter, for eyes

Stitch marker, fiberfill stuffing, tapestry needle

2 wooden buttons, for overalls

» Sailor's Hat

With white, make a magic circle (page 61).

Rnd 1: Work 7 sc in ring.

Rnd 2: *Hdc 2 in next sc; rep from * around—14 sts.

Rnd 3: (Hdc in next st, 2 hdc in next st) 7 times—21 sts.

Rnd 4: (Hdc in each of next 2 sts, 2 hdc in next st) 7 times—28 sts.

Rnd 5: (Hdc in each of next 3 sts, 2 hdc in next st) 7 times—35 sts.

Rnd 6: (Hdc in each of next 4 sts, 2 hdc in next st) 7 times—42 sts.

Rnd 7: (Hdc in each of next 5 sts, 2 hdc in next st) 7 times—49 sts.

Rnd 8: (Hdc in each of next 6 sts, 2 hdc in next st) 7 times—56 sts.

Rnd 9: (Hdc in each of next 7 sts, 2 hdc in next st) 7 times—63 sts.

Rnds 10–13: Sc around.

Rnd 14: (Sc in each of next 7 sts, sc2tog) 7 times—56 sts.

Rnds 15–18: Sc around.

Rnd 19: Through front loops only, (sc in each of next 7 sts, 2 sc in following st) 7 times—63 sts.

Rnd 20: Sc around.

Rnd 21: With navy, (sc in each of next 8 sts, 2 sc in following st) 7 times—70 sts.

Rnd 22: Sc around.

Rnd 23: With white, (sc in each of next 9 sts, 2 sc in following st) 7 times—77 sts.

Rnd 24: Sc around.

Rnd 25: With navy, (sc in each of next 10 sts, 2 sc in following st) 7 times—84 sts.

Rnd 26: Sc around.

Rnd 27: With white, (sc in each of next 11 sts, 2 sc in following st) 7 times—91 sts.

Rnd 28: Sl st around.

Fasten off, leaving a long tail for sewing.

» Ears

Make 2.

With white, make a magic circle.

Rnd 1: Work 6 sc in ring.

Rnd 2: *Sc 2 in next sc; rep from * around—12 sts.

Rnd 3: (Sc in next st, 2 sc in following st) 6 times—18 sts.

Rnd 4: (Sc in each of next 2 sts, 2 sc in following st) 6 times—24 sts.

Sew the hat to the head over one ear.

Rnd 5: (Sc in each of next 3 sts, 2 sc in following st) 6 times—30 sts.

Rnd 6: (Sc in each of next 4 sts, 2 sc in following st) 6 times—36 sts.

Rnds 7–10: Sc around.

Rnd 11: (Sc in each of next 4 sts, sc2tog) 6 times—30 sts.

Rnd 12: (Sc in each of next 3 sts, sc2tog) 6 times—24 sts.

Fasten off, leaving a long tail for sewing.

» Muzzle

With white, make a magic circle.

Rnd 1: Work 6 sc in ring.

Rnd 2: *Sc 2 in next sc; rep from * around—12 sts.

Rnd 3: (Sc in next st, 2 sc in following st) 6 times—18 sts.

Rnd 4: (Sc in each of next 2 sts, 2 sc in following st) 6 times—24 sts.

Rnd 5: (Sc in each of next 3 sts, 2 sc in following st) 6 times—30 sts.

Rnd 6: (Sc in each of next 4 sts, 2 sc in following st) 6 times—36 sts.

Rnd 7: (Sc in each of next 5 sts, 2 sc in following st) 6 times—42 sts.

Rnd 8: Sc around.

Fasten off, leaving a long tail for sewing.

» Head

With off-white, make a magic circle.

Rnd 1: Work 6 sc in ring.

Rnd 2: *Sc 2 in next sc; rep from * around—12 sts.

Rnd 3: (Sc in next st, 2 sc in following st) 6 times—18 sts.

Rnd 4: (Sc in each of next 2 sts, 2 sc in following st) 6 times—24 sts.

Rnd 5: (Sc in each of next 3 sts, 2 sc in following st) 6 times—30 sts.

Rnd 6: (Sc in each of next 4 sts, 2 sc in following st) 6 times—36 sts.

Rnd 7: (Sc in each of next 5 sts, 2 sc in following st) 6 times—42 sts.

Rnd 8: (Sc in each of next 6 sts, 2 sc in following st) 6 times—48 sts.

Rnd 9: (Sc in each of next 7 sts, 2 sc in following st) 6 times—54 sts.

Rnd 10: (Sc in each of next 8 sts, 2 sc in following st) 6 times—60 sts.

Rnd 11: (Sc in each of next 9 sts, 2 sc in following st) 6 times—66 sts.

Rnd 12: (Sc in each of next 10 sts, 2 sc in following st) 6 times—72 sts.

Rnd 13: (Sc in each of next 11 sts, 2 sc in following st) 6 times—78 sts.

Rnd 14: (Sc in each of next 12 sts, 2 sc in following st) 6 times—84 sts.

Rnd 15: (Sc in each of next 13 sts, 2 sc in following st) 6 times—90 sts.

Rnd 16: (Sc in each of next 14 sts, 2 sc in following st) 6 times—96 sts.

Rnds 17–28: Sc around.

Rnd 29: (Sc in each of next 15 sts, 2 sc in following st) 6 times—102 sts.

Rnd 30: Sc around.

Rnd 31: (Sc in each of next 15 sts, sc2tog) 6 times—96 sts.

Rnd 32: (Sc in each of next 14 sts, sc2tog) 6 times—90 sts.

Rnd 33: (Sc in each of next 13 sts, sc2tog) 6 times—84 sts.

Rnd 34: (Sc in each of next 12 sts, sc2tog) 6 times—78 sts.

Rnd 35: (Sc in each of next 11 sts, sc2tog) 6 times—72 sts.

Rnd 36: (Sc in each of next 10 sts, sc2tog) 6 times—66 sts.

Rnd 37: (Sc in each of next 9 sts, sc2tog) 6 times—60 sts.

Rnd 38: (Sc in each of next 8 sts, sc2tog) 6 times—54 sts.

Rnd 39: (Sc in each of next 7 sts, sc2tog) 6 times—48 sts.

Rnd 40: (Sc in each of next 6 sts, sc2tog) 6 times—42 sts.

Rnd 41: (Sc in each of next 5 sts, sc2tog) 6 times—36 sts.

Fasten off.

» Body

With navy, make a magic circle.

Rnd 1: Work 6 sc in ring.

Rnd 2: (Sc in each of next 2 sts, 2 sc in following st) 2 times—8 sts.

Rnd 3: *Sc 2 in next sc; rep from * around—16 sts.

Rnd 4: (Sc in next st, 2 sc in following st) 8 times—24 sts.

Rnd 5: (Sc in each of next 2 sts, 2 sc in following st) 8 times—32 sts.

Rnd 6: (Sc in each of next 3 sts, 2 sc in following st) 8 times—40 sts.

Rnd 7: (Sc in each of next 4 sts, 2 sc in following st) 8 times—48 sts.

Rnd 8: (Sc in each of next 5 sts, 2 sc in following st) 8 times—56 sts.

Rnd 9: (Sc in each of next 6 sts, 2 sc in following st) 8 times—64 sts.

Rnd 10: (Sc in each of next 7 sts, 2 sc in following st) 8 times—72 sts.

Rnd 11: (Sc in each of next 8 sts, 2 sc in following st) 8 times—80 sts.

Rnds 12–16: Sc around.

Rnd 17: (Sc in each of next 8 sts, sc2tog) 8 times—72 sts.

Rnds 18 and 19: Sc around.

Rnd 20: (Sc in each of next 7 sts, sc2tog) 8 times—64 sts.

Rnd 21: Sc around.

Rnd 22: With white, through back loops only, sc around.

Rnds 23 and 24: Sc around.

Rnd 25: (Sc in each of next 6 sts, sc2tog) 8 times—56 sts.

Rnds 26–30: Sc around.

Rnd 31: (Sc in each of next 5 sts, sc2tog) 8 times—48 sts.

Rnds 32–34: Sc around.

Rnd 35: (Sc in each of next 4 sts, sc2tog) 8 times—40 sts.

Fasten off, leaving a long tail for sewing.

» Arms

Make 2.

With off-white, make a magic circle.

Rnd 1: Work 5 sc in ring.

Rnd 2: *Sc 2 in next sc; rep from * around—10 sts.

Rnd 3: (Sc in next st, 2 sc in following st) 5 times—15 sts.

Rnd 4: (Sc in each of next 2 sts, 2 sc in following st) 5 times—20 sts.

Rnd 5: (Sc in each of next 3 sts, 2 sc in following st) 5 times—25 sts.

Rnd 6: (Sc in each of next 4 sts, 2 sc in following st) 5 times—30 sts.

Rnd 7: Sc around.

Rnd 8: With white, through front loops only, sc around. Through back loops only of same rnd, (sc in each of next 4 sts, sc2tog) 5 times—25 sts.

Rnd 9: Sc around.

Rnd 10: With navy, sc around.

Rnd 11: With white, sc around.

Rnd 12: With navy, (sc in each of next 3 sts, sc2tog) 5 times—20 sts.

Rnds 13–15: With white, sc around.

Rnd 16: (Sc in each of next 2 sts, sc2tog) 5 times—15 sts.

Rnds 17–21: Sc around.

Fasten off, leaving a long tail for sewing.

»Legs

Make 2.

With white, ch 8.

Rnd 1: Sc in 2nd ch from hook and in each of next 2 ch, hdc in each of next 4 ch. Turn foundation ch. On opposite side of foundation ch, hdc in each of next 4 ch, sc in each of rem 3 ch—14 sts.

Rnd 2: Sc in each of next 4 sts, hdc in next st, 2 hdc in each of next 6 sts, sc in each of rem 3 sts—20 sts.

Rnd 3: Sc in each of next 3 sts, 2 sc in next st, hdc in each of next 3 sts, 2 hdc in next st, dc in each of next 3 sts, 2 dc in next st, hdc in each of next 3 sts, 2 hdc in next st, sc in each of next 3 sts, 2 sc in last st—25 sts.

Rnd 4: Sc in each of next 10 sts, 2 sc in each of next 5 sts, sc in each of next 10 sts—30 sts.

Rnd 5: Through back loops only, sc around.

Rnd 6: Sc in each of next 10 sts, sc2tog 5 times, sc in each of rem 10 sts—25 sts.

Rnd 7: Sc in each of next 7 sts, sc2tog 5 times, sc in each of next 8 sts—20 sts.

Rnd 8: Sc in each of next 8 sts, sc2tog 2 times, sc in each of next 8 sts—18 sts.

Rnd 9: With off-white, through back loops only, sc around.

Rnds 10 and 11: Sc around.

Rnd 12: With navy, through front loops only, (sc in each of next 8 sts, 2 sc in following st) 2 times—20 sts.

Rnd 13: Sc around.

Rnd 14: (Sc in each of next 3 sts, 2 sc in following st) 5 times—25 sts.

Rnds 15 and 16: Sc around.

Fasten off, leaving a long tail for sewing.

»Overall Straps

Make 2.

With navy, ch 53.

Row 1: Hdc in 3rd ch from hook and in each ch across—51 sts.

Fasten off, leaving a long tail for sewing.

Side view.

Cross the straps in the back before sewing the ends in place.

»Assembly

Fold brim of hat up along rnd 19. Stuff. Sew hat and ears to head. With pink, embroider a "T" on muzzle for a nose. Stuff muzzle and sew to head. Sew eyes in place. Stuff arms and legs. Sew arms and legs to body. Sew a wooden button to each overall strap. Sew straps to body, crossing in back with buttons in front. Stuff head and body. Sew head to body. Weave in ends.

Crochet Basics

Following is some basic information for making the toys in this book. If you need more details, go to ShopMartingale.com/HowtoCrochet for free, downloadable instructions. For more tips, see "Tips and Tricks" on page 31.

» SAFETY FIRST

Small parts, like beads, plastic eyes, and buttons, aren't suitable for toys intended for small children since they're a choking hazard. If the amigurumi is a gift for a young child, you can substitute embroidered eyes instead.

» Tools

When making amigurumi, I find it more comfortable to use a hook with a soft grip around the handle to lessen the pressure on my fingers. I usually use the Hamanaka brand size 6/0 or regular F-5 (3.75 mm) crochet hooks, but I sometimes like to change to a larger or smaller size hook to change the size of the finished project.

To keep track of the start of each round, I use a stitch marker. If you don't have a stitch marker handy, don't worry, just grab a safety pin and you're good to go! Place the stitch marker on the very first stitch of the round and just move it after each round is completed. Also make sure to have a tapestry needle and pins (if desired)—these will be your best friends in sewing your amigurumi just right.

When making amigurumi, a popular choice is to use safety eyes, but it is not always so easy to find them. A fun alternative is to use buttons or flat-bottomed jewels. Unlike safety eyes, buttons and jewels give added character and an extra pop of color to your amigurumi. Buttons are sewn in place, while a tacky glue can be used to secure jewels.

And of course, what would amigurumi be without stuffing? Go to your local yarn or craft shop to purchase fiberfill; however, if you don't have any on hand, simply make use of any old pillows that you don't use.

» Yarns

Most of the amigurumi were made using a high-bulk 4-ply acrylic yarn brand not available outside the Philippines. Don't worry about finding the exact yarn since the patterns are still workable using different yarns. Select any smooth, DK-weight acrylic yarn for the projects in this book. This type of yarn tends to come in a rainbow of colors, so finding what you need should be a snap! Of course, worsted or other weights of yarn can be used as well, just be certain to adjust the hook size to achieve a firm fabric (and remember that changing the yarn and hook will affect the finished size of the project).

» Gauge and Tension

All of the finished sizes in this book are based solely on how I crochet and my gauge. Yours may come out bigger or smaller, but don't fret. The beauty of amigurumi is that you don't really need to follow a gauge so long as your tension remains consistent throughout. Aim for a firm but not-too-dense fabric, that will hold its shape without being floppy or allowing the stuffing to show between the stitches.

» Working in Rounds

Each amigurumi here is worked in the round unless otherwise stated. Unless otherwise noted, rounds are worked continuously in a spiral, never joined with a slip stitch.

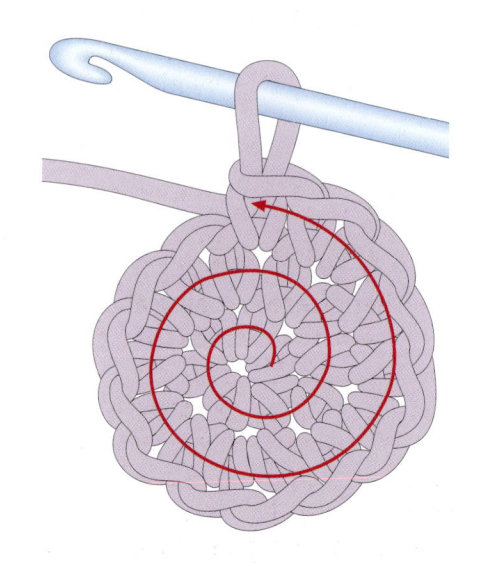

Crochet Basics

» Closing Up Ends

When working with amigurumi, one important question is *how do I close the amigurumi on the final round so that the stuffing won't fall out?* First, take a tapestry needle and thread the yarn tail. Then, insert the needle in the next stitch from the outside in and continue around, weaving in and out through each stitch on the last round. Pull the tail firmly and the stitches will close in, like tightening a drawstring. Secure the end and trim, allowing the end of the tail to hide in the stuffing.

» Sewing Pieces Together

Whenever possible, use tails left at the end of a row or round to sew pieces together; this saves time and energy. If the tail is not long enough, cut a new length of yarn and thread it on a tapestry needle. If desired, pin the pieces to be joined to align them perfectly, then sew together neatly using whipstitch.

» Stitches and Techniques

Another awesome thing about making amigurumi is that it makes use of basic stitches and techniques, so these projects are great for newer crocheters! Single crochet is used most often, though taller stitches are used for shaping. Most pieces begin with a magic circle, explained here.

MAGIC CIRCLE

The magic circle technique (also known as an adjustable loop) is a simple way to begin crocheting in rounds. Loop the yarn around your index finger and pinch to form a loop, leaving a 4" tail. With hook, draw the working yarn through the loop and ch 1, removing your finger. Next, follow the pattern instructions to work the required number of stitches around the ring for the next round, then pull the tail snugly to close. You can use your finger to keep the loop open while making your first stitch.

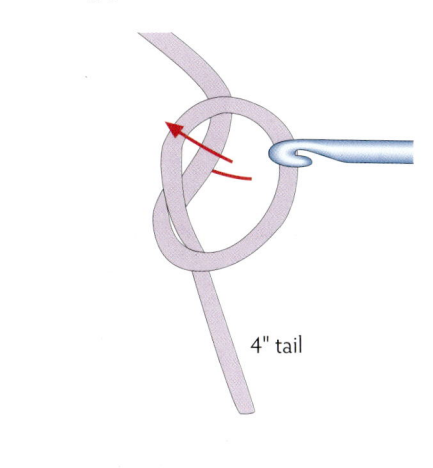

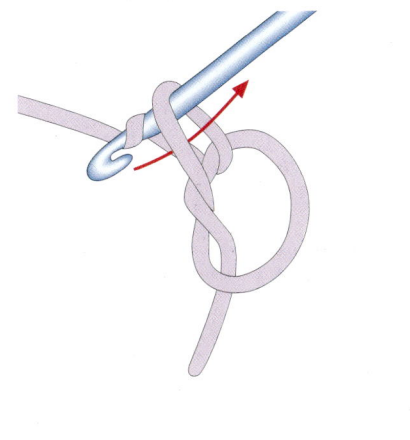

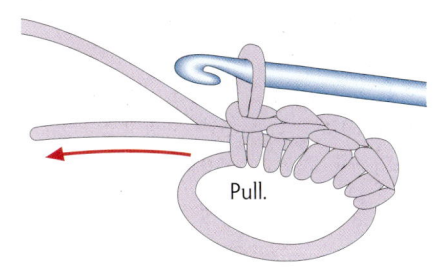

4" tail

Pull.

CHAIN [CH]

Wrap the yarn around the hook and then pull the hook through the loop to create a chain stitch.

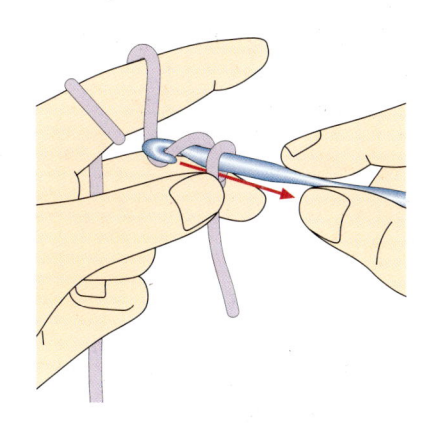

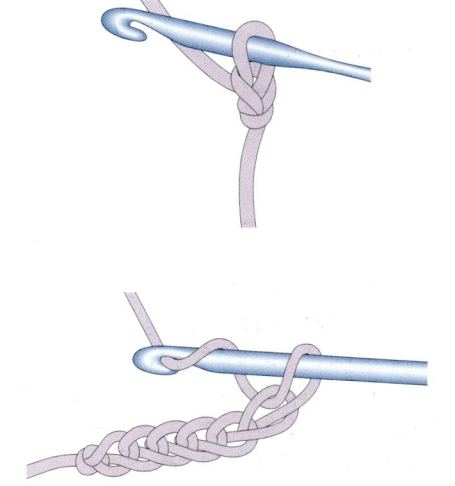

SLIP STITCH [SL ST]

Insert the hook in the indicated chain or stitch. Wrap the yarn around the hook, draw through both loops on the hook.

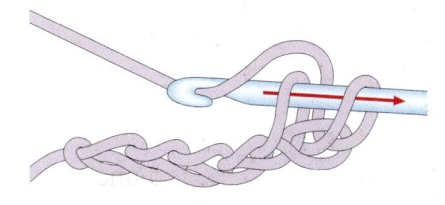

Huggable Amigurumi

SINGLE CROCHET [SC]

Insert the hook in the indicated chain or stitch. Wrap the yarn around the hook, draw up a loop; wrap the yarn around the hook, draw through both loops on the hook.

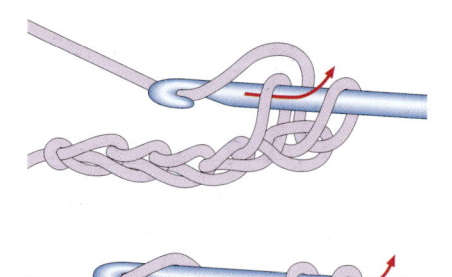

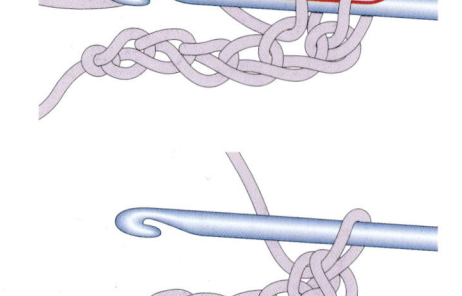

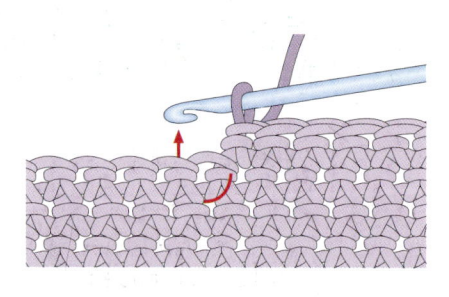

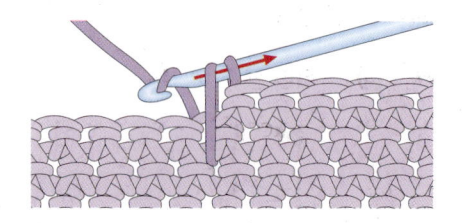

HALF DOUBLE CROCHET [HDC]

Yarn over the hook, then insert the hook in the indicated chain or stitch. Wrap the yarn around the hook, draw up a loop; wrap the yarn around the hook, draw through all loops on the hook.

LONG SINGLE CROCHET [LONG SC]

Work as for single crochet, inserting the hook in the stitch of the row below.

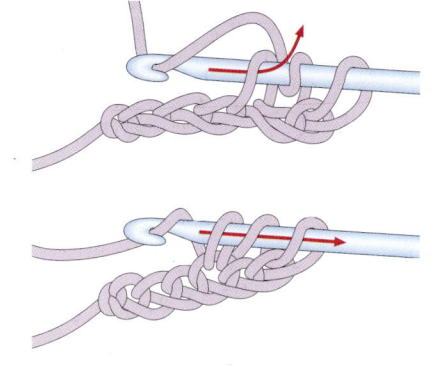

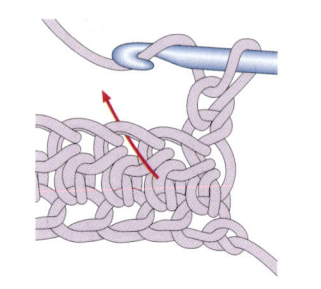

DOUBLE CROCHET [DC]

Yarn over the hook, then insert the hook in the indicated chain or stitch. Wrap the yarn around the hook, draw up a loop; (wrap the yarn around the hook, draw through two loops on the hook) twice.

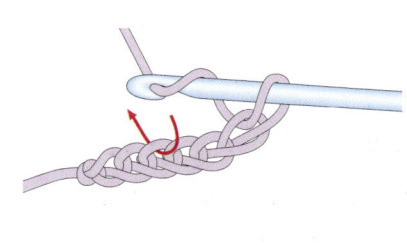

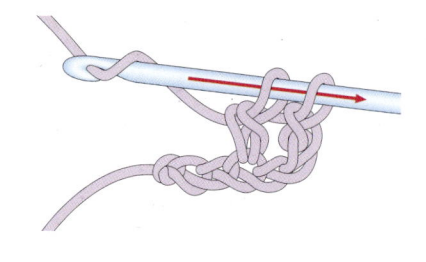

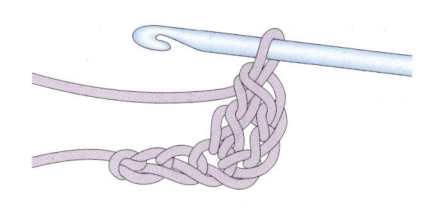

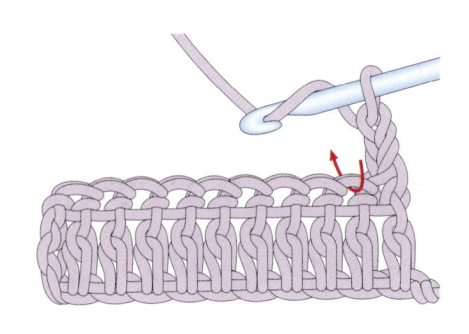

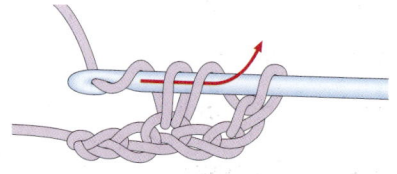

PUFF STITCH

Working in the same stitch, (yarn over the hook, then insert the hook in the indicated chain or stitch. Wrap the yarn around the hook, draw up a loop) four times so there are nine loops on the hook. Yarn over and draw through all loops on the hook, ch1.

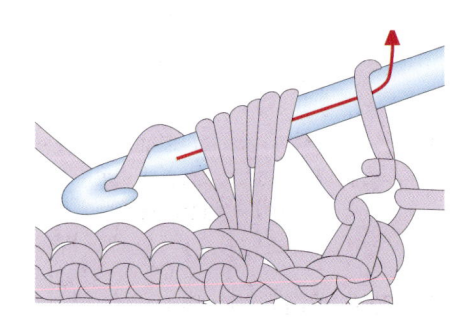

CROCHETING TWO STITCHES TOGETHER

When crocheting two stitches together, regardless of whether they are single, double, or any other type of crochet stitch, the process is the same. Work the first stitch until two loops remain on the hook, then work the second stitch to the same point (in other words, do not make the last "yarn over, draw through two loops" of each stitch). Once both stitches are worked to this point, yarn over and draw through the remaining loops of both stitches, joining them into a single stitch.

INCREASE
To increase, simply work two stitches in the same stitch or space.

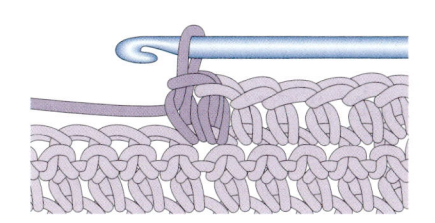

DECREASE [SC2TOG]
Throughout this book, decreases are worked as single crochet two together (sc2tog). To make the decrease less visible, work through the front loops only.

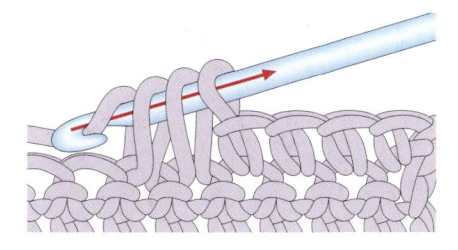

LOOPS
Most amigurumi here is worked using both loops of the crochet stitch. However, there are exceptions. When indicated, you will work stitches through the front or back loops only.

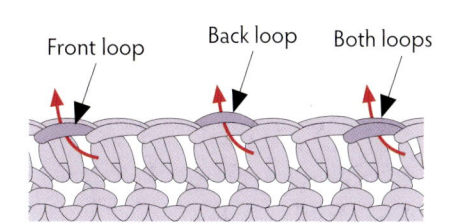

Front loop   Back loop   Both loops

COLOR CHANGE
There are many ways to change yarn colors, but the neatest way I've seen is to work the last stitch before the color change until two loops remain on the hook, then join the new yarn to complete the stitch.

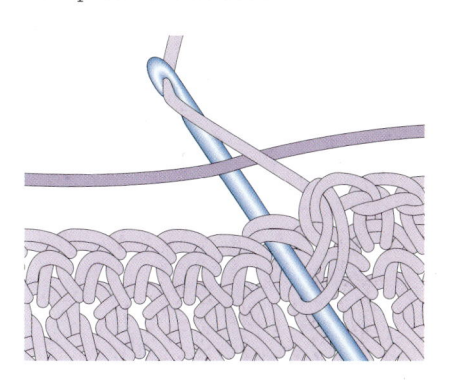

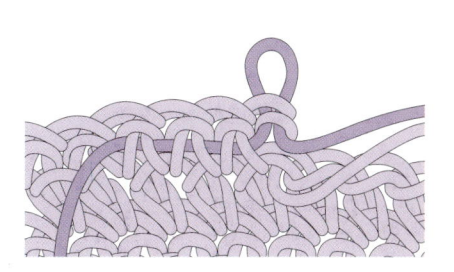

» Abbreviations »

( )	Work instructions within parentheses as many times as directed.	dec(s)	decrease(ing)(s)	sc	single crochet(s)
		hdc	half double crochet(s)	sc2tog	single crochet 2 stitches together— 1 stitch decreased
		inc(s)	increase(ing)(s)		
approx	approximately	long sc	long single crochet(s)		
beg	begin(ning)	mm	millimeter(s)	sk	skip
ch	chain(s) or chain stitch(es)	prev	previous	sl st(s)	slip stitch(es)
		rem	remain(ing)	sp(s)	space(s)
cont	continue(ing)(s)	rep(s)	repeat(s)	st(s)	stitch(es)
dc	double crochet(s)	rnd(s)	round(s)	tog	together

» About the Author »

Shannen is a college student and amigurumi designer who lives in the Philippines. She started crocheting as a school requirement in the sixth grade and fell in love with the craft. By the time she was in her second year of high school, she learned about amigurumi, which made her love crocheting even more. Her love of animals contributes to her amigurumi designs, as she tries to make all her dream animals come to life—well, in plushie form. Since 2011, she has been posting all her amigurumi creations to her various social networking sites and selling patterns online.

You can follow Shannen through social media at the following addresses.

f   http://facebook.com/SweetNCuteCreations

t   http://SweetNCuteCreations.tumblr.com

🐦 📷   @SNCxCreations

» Acknowledgments »

First off, **thank you** for buying this book.

Many, many thanks to everyone who has supported my crochet dream by always believing in me. Thanks to my dad for being both my #1 critic and #1 supporter. Thanks to the rest of my family for being supportive of my hobby. Thank you to all my friends for being so enthusiastic whenever I make something new. To all my teachers, both crafts and non-crafts, thank you for instilling in me values and skills that have helped me complete this book. Thank you to all my fans and crochet friends on social media for keeping me inspired and for helping me make design decisions.

And of course, thank you to Karen Burns and the entire team at Martingale for making this dream of mine a reality. ♥♥♥

What's your creative passion?

Find it at ShopMartingale.com

books • eBooks • ePatterns • daily blog • free projects
videos • tutorials • inspiration • giveaways

Martingale®
Create with Confidence